Finding
Strength,
Spirit
+
Personal
Power

REACH!

LAILA ALI

with

DAVID RITZ

HYPERION

New York

ISBN: 0-7868-6855-4

Hyperion books are available for special promotions and premi-
ums. For details contact Hyperion Special Markets, 77 West 66th
Street, 11th floor, New York, New York 10023, or call 212-456-0100.

Book design by Lorelle Graffeo

FIRST EDITION

10   9   8   7   6   5   4   3   2   1

For all

young women

searching for

self-fulfillment

LAILA'S
ACKNOWLEDGMENTS:

I want to thank my husband for his support and unconditional love; my mother, Hana, and Carl for always telling me the truth; my dad for being the greatest; David Ritz, Al Hassas, Dub Huntley, Cassius Green, the staff of Girls Republic, Judge Dorn, Nisaa Siefullah.

DAVID'S
ACKNOWLEDGMENTS:

I want to thank Laila, for her honesty and confidence in me; Dan Strone, Brenda Urban, Mark Chait, Will Schwalbe, Maureen O'Brien, Al Hassas, Yahya McClain, Veronica Porche Anderson, Carl Anderson, Nicola Goode, my loving wife Roberta and wonderful daughters Alison and Jessica. And special thanks to my dear friend Alan Eisenstock for strong and steady support.

Round 1

OWNING

YOUR

OWN STORY

Everyone's story is special. And I believe everyone's story deserves attention. Before I begin, though, I'd like to tell you why I'm telling my story.

At first I hesitated. I've always been a little suspicious of people who write books the minute they get famous. It doesn't matter if they really have anything to say; the point is only to increase their fame. That's the last thing I wanted to do. I told myself, *if I write a book, it's going to have to mean something; it's going to have to help people—and tell the truth.*

The truth is that my own celebrity is a source of conflict. When I started boxing, I realized the name of the game is winning. The more wins, the more fame. I also knew my famous name was an advantage. But as you'll soon see, fame never attracted me as a child, or as a teenager, or even as a young adult. I associated fame with false friends, fake behavior, and hangers-on. Raised around fame, I saw its downside—and

1

moved in the opposite direction. My close friends were regular people, not celebrities. I lived a life that was private, where no one really cared about my famous family.

My decision to fight changed all that. That decision wasn't easy. To this day, it remains challenging. I'm still adjusting to a public life that often makes me uncomfortable. My essential shyness is still there. I still avoid celebrity parties and high-profile Hollywood gatherings. But reality is reality, and the plain fact is that I've achieved a small dose of fame. The plain fact is also that I'm motivated to inspire others.

I want to do so by honestly describing what I've been through. I can't call this book my life story because, at twenty-four, my life has just begun. At the same time, my youth gives me a unique advantage; my experiences are still fresh. I'm still challenged by decisions on every level—emotional, occupational, spiritual—that young people (and not-so-young people) face every day.

My shyness has kept me from saying much in public. In my interviews, I tend to hold back. Journalists can twist words and take them out of context. Journalists can also provoke rash remarks. So I lay back and keep my comments clipped. A thirty-second sound bite isn't the ideal forum for meaningful self-expression. But a book is. Written from the heart, a book is the best way to show you who I am. And make an impact.

I don't want to exaggerate or overdramatize. I know many people have had a much harder time than I have. And there are those who have had it easier. Comparisons don't prove anything. My point is neither to lament how my life has been rough nor boast how my life has been privileged. I simply want to speak directly to you and share my heartaches, joys, failures, and victories.

I believe I have a gift.

I believe everyone has a gift.

The struggle is in finding the gift, believing in the gift, and allowing the gift to shape our lives. That wasn't easy for me. Like my father, I'm stubborn by nature. Being headstrong has gotten me into trouble and landed me in dangerous situations. I'm not always a fast learner. But when I do learn something, it sticks. I want to tell you what I've learned, not by lecturing but by example. I want you to get to know me.

People are always saying, "You're so pretty. Why don't you just model or act? Why do you want to box?"

This book explains why—why I had to find a path that was right for me, and why we all need to find our own paths. We only have one life to live. When we allow society to define us— as in, *pretty girls shouldn't box*—we never find that special gift within us. We wind up frustrated, lost, and unhappy.

I know a lot of women judge themselves harshly. Often we're our own worst critic. We tend to beat up on ourselves, blaming ourselves for everything that goes wrong. I'm blessed in being able to avoid that attitude. I don't judge myself and, in this book, I won't judge my story. I also won't judge the people with whom I've interacted. I don't mean that I love everyone who has come my way, but I've come to see everyone has a purpose in my life. They're there to teach me something, if only I'm clear and open enough to learn the lesson.

I've met people who presume I've always been successful. Because I come from a successful family, they think success came naturally. It didn't. I have had to work hard for whatever I've accomplished. I'm still working hard. My success hasn't been easy. My parents, for all their wonderful qualities, didn't give me a lot of guidance. The guidance I found was hidden deep inside. I saw that guidance when I started taking responsibility for myself—and owning my own story.

That means telling it straight, without sugarcoating or excuses. I don't need to sweeten my story, and I don't need to sensationalize it. I simply need to accept it. By accepting it, I'm no longer helpless. I can go on and write a new chapter. I can even take the story to another level. I can be in charge—and not the victim of old circumstances. That's what it means to reach beyond our circumstances, to reach higher and accomplish more.

I believe it all starts with ourselves. That's not being selfish; that's being real. If it's wisdom we want to extend to others, we first have to attain wisdom for ourselves. If we view our past clearly, we have a decent shot at clearly viewing our present— and forging our future in the light of good sense and love.

Ever since I was a little girl, I've been called an old soul. Something about me made people say I was mature beyond my years. But being an old soul didn't prevent me from making mistakes.

We're on this earth to make mistakes. The goal is to learn from those mistakes.

For the sake of clarity, I'm dividing my stories into rounds and pointing out the positive lessons I've learned. Not that I learned in time to avoid the mistakes. You'll see how I messed up. The lessons are there to remind myself—and, I hope, you too—that positive power is all around us, if only we recognize it. The lessons aren't laws or rules but guideposts, little signs to remind us that even out of heartbreak, *especially* out of heartbreak, we find ways to be strong.

So I'm shining the light on my past. I'm going back to the

beginning. I'm telling you the story of how a pretty little girl, born inside a fairy tale, went through life's lost-and-found. I experienced all the stuff kids and teens and young adults experience. I hurt others and I hurt myself. I got into trouble. And I don't apologize for any of it. It's my journey. All I can do is share it with you and thank you for coming along for the ride.

Round 2

ACCEPTING YOUR PARENTS FOR WHO THEY ARE

A *four-year-old girl is running away from home.*

She throws her clothes and a bunch of junk into a plastic garbage bag and starts screaming, "I'm going! I'm going far, far away!" She dashes out of her house, only to have her mother dash after her. The little girl makes it past the front door and hurries down the street, dragging the garbage bag behind her, when she turns and sees her mother gaining on her. Her mother is running in high heels, her long hair blowing in the afternoon breeze.

"Laila," says the mother. "Where do you think you're going?"

"I'm going away."

"Why, honey?"

"Just because."

With her head hung down, the daughter stares at the ground. She feels her mother's gentle caress against her cheek. She feels better. Finally she has what she has wanted all along—her mother's attention.

Someone looking back at my childhood might wonder how I could ever have been unhappy. My father was a hero to millions of people; my mother was looked on as one of the most beautiful women in the world. We lived in a private gated community, in an enormous four-story mansion with a full staff of nannies, maids, and cooks. It looked like I had everything a child could want, and more. But looks are deceptive. The one thing I didn't have was the very thing kids need most—a feeling that everything was all right. Security.

Looking back, my mother and father were not close. On the surface, they seemed the perfect couple, but their differences kept them apart. The public image was one thing, but the personal reality was something entirely different.

My folks were into appearances. I don't mean that negatively. Most public people have to be into appearances because their every move is scrutinized. At the same time, they wanted their private business to remain private. That's why they lived together as long as they did, even when their marriage, for all practical purposes, had fallen apart. For the last two years I lived in my father's house, I didn't know my parents were separated. They chose to maintain the image of togetherness. At the same time, I felt the unease. Kids sense stuff, and I sensed a lot.

We were a four-member family who lived in Fremont Place, an exclusive enclave in the middle of Los Angeles. It was me, my sister Hana (a year and a half older than me), my mom, and my dad. I have six step-siblings from Dad's past wives. He had been married twice before, and his other kids, all older than us, would visit from time to time.

My mother, Veronica Porche, met Muhammad at his height, in 1974, when he beat Joe Frazier and George Foreman. They married soon after. Mom was barely out of her teens, Dad in his early thirties. Hana and me, the baby of the family born December 30, 1977, are the only kids of Muhammad and Veronica.

Hana was a daddy's girl. I wasn't. I was quiet and shy—my parents say I was sweet—and from time to time could be a little dramatic. I threatened to do crazy things like jump off the roof and kill myself. The threats, though, really weren't serious. The feeling I most remember is loneliness.

My discomfort was subtle. In many ways, my parents were wonderful, which made my own conflicted feelings about them even more confusing. Above the conflicts, the fundamental fact of my childhood is this: I was never that close to my father. I was never as comfortable with him as I was with Mom.

I remember approaching my father in his study, a huge room with a fireplace and big-screen TV. I hated going in there because it was always packed with people I didn't know—advisers, friends, fans, hangers-on. They hung on his every word as he sat behind his mammoth antique desk. He did magic tricks and everyone marveled. He told jokes and everyone laughed. He was cool in this context because he liked being the center of attention. By calling me to him, he drew me into that center, which is exactly where I didn't want to be. I looked around at this roomful of strangers. Yes, I wanted attention, but not from people I didn't know. Who were they? Were they real or fake?

When my father made me sit on his lap, everyone oohed and aahed about how cute I was. I knew Daddy was a big-hearted man who adored children. I knew he adored me. But it didn't feel comfortable being adored. He'd smother me with sloppy kisses. I didn't like that stuff. I didn't want my cheeks pinched by people I didn't know.

"Hana never complains about me kissing her," he'd say.

"Then give her all the kisses."

And with that, I'd run from the room.

My father was a people person. That's where he got his energy and how he expressed his love.

He loved to praise. He'd say you were the greatest cook in the world, the greatest writer, the greater golfer or caddy or actor or plumber. He loved making people feel good. He loved piling us in the back of his Rolls-Royce convertible and, with the top down, ride down Wilshire Boulevard, putting himself and his kids on full display.

He'd start off by saying, "I'm killing us all!" and, with that, stomp down on the gas pedal and go roaring off.

"No, Daddy, no!" we'd yell, half giddy, half afraid.

His assistant sitting next to him would turn green with fright. Now I see it as stupid and dangerous; back then I saw it as fun. Daddy was one of us, a big kid.

People would shout, "There's Ali! He's the greatest!" People loved recognizing him, and Daddy loved the attention. He'd drive with one hand on the wheel and wave with the other, smiling all the way. If he saw a homeless person on the corner, he'd stop and give money. If the person was crippled or disfigured, my father might shed tears. At the sight of someone less fortunate than himself, he would remind us of how blessed we were to have our health. At the Carnation Coffee Shop or Bob's Big Boy, he'd let us order whatever we wanted—a whole dinner of desserts. Crowds flocked around us as he freely gave autographs, advice, photos. I'd seen him leave waitresses hundred-dollar tips. I'd also seen him get distracted and forget us, actually leave the restaurant and have to return to fetch his kids.

Daddy was an overgrown child. He liked putting on Halloween masks and chasing us around the house. He knew we hated vegetables, so at dinnertime, when the nanny wasn't looking, he'd scoop the broccoli off our plates and eat it for us. He'd swallow our huge vitamins so we wouldn't have to. He'd rescue, protect, and spoil us any way he could. Mainly, though, he just wanted to slobber kisses on us and make sure we were observant Muslims. My dad gave us lots of love. His only requirement was that we grow up respectful Muslim women.

I resisted his kisses as well as his religion. I dreaded those early mornings when he woke us up and led us into our living room, which felt as big as a bowling alley, to repeat foreign words I didn't understand. We'd recite the prayers over and again. I waited for the moment when we could bow and rest our heads on the carpet so I could close my eyes and sleep. I never felt pious or inspired, only tired. My only prayer was for the prayer session to end so I could go back to bed.

I disliked the mosque even more. Daddy would take us there and turn us over to the sisters. Men sat in front, women in back. I was restless and bored and didn't understand what was being said. Many times Daddy left without us. Again, he'd forget us—not out of malice, but simply because that was his way.

His religious way was deep—I realize that now—but when he pulled us out of our elementary school and put us in a Muslim school, I was miserable. I missed my friends from the neighborhood. The religious instruction went over my head. Mom saw we weren't learning anything and insisted we return to our original school.

I never heard my parents fight, but their separate bedrooms said it all. Looking back, I understand that separateness. Dad ran an open household. He invited the outside world in. All you had to do was go to the gatehouse and tell the guard you were there to see Ali. Dad couldn't refuse anyone. He'd take you on a tour of his home and show you all his trophies. He thrived on having company, night and day, and, as a natural-born entertainer, loved to please. He also loved to travel and was often off on trips. But whether he was there or not, it felt like our house was open to the public.

That's one reason why my mother kept her door closed. I could imagine she wasn't comfortable—and didn't feel safe—in such an open atmosphere. When she married, she had had little life experience and was hardly her own person. She probably had no idea what she was getting into. Even more importantly, she had fallen deeply in love. He was, after all, enormously powerful and charming; he genuinely cared for her. As she matured as a woman, though, the differences between them widened dramatically. My dad's ideals were set by his religion. Women were to behave in certain ways, but, more and more, those ways didn't fit my mother.

She was more than a strikingly

beautiful woman; she was also highly intelligent.

And even though she had agreed to drop out of college and abandon plans to become a doctor, her growing independence was a factor that neither she nor Dad could ignore.

Mom's parents were Catholics who had separated. "I never formally converted to Islam," she told me many years later. "Before we married, your father simply asked, 'Do you submit to the will of God?' I said, 'Yes.' 'Then,' he assured me, 'you're already a Muslim.' "

Their courtship was lightning fast. Everyone urged her to marry him. How could any woman in her right mind *not* marry him? Moreover, she loved Muhammad mightily. This all happened in the seventies, when my father was at his height. Later, when I had to write book reports for school and, out of laziness, chose him as my subject, I'd learn a little about his famous fights. But I was never intrigued by his career and, to be honest, never got caught up in his superstardom.

Strikingly tall and always elegant, Mom was a star in her own right. Her position as Ali's wife made her famous.

To the world, Mom and Dad were royalty, perfect physical specimens, the ideal couple.

He was a king, she his queen. But she had ideas and an identity of her own. She wasn't born to be a passive housewife. Moreover, Mom's sense of fashion didn't conform to the Muslim code.

Hana related to my father. I identified with Mom. I was often in my mother's enormous bedroom. There was a marble fireplace, billowing drapes, big overstuffed chairs, a walk-in dressing room, and walk-in closets for her fabulous wardrobe. Hana and I would sit on an antique bench in front of her bed and close our eyes until she said, "Surprise!" She'd give us glass dolls adorned in exquisite dresses. She'd let us try on her clothes, put on her makeup, indulge us in the art of dressing up.

The feeling of femininity in the room was enchanting. She showered us with love, and we soaked it up. Our little private moments will stay with me forever. I can still see her crystal decanters on a tray next to her bed and smell her sweet perfumes. She was loving but preoccupied, engaged in a thousand activities, yet as long as I was close to her the world could do me no harm.

Unlike Dad, though, Mom was not touchy-feely. She had a special diet and her own eating schedule. Aside from Thanksgiving, I don't remember ever eating meals as a family. Mom was always watching her weight; her self-discipline was strict. She was always hurrying off to aerobics class and vocal lessons. The door to her bedroom was usually closed, which meant, of course, do not disturb. I might hear her singing scales or practicing arias; she loved opera. She had no interest in cooking and, for that matter, didn't have to keep tabs on what or whether we ate. We had cooks and nannies to worry about that.

Hana could be disobedient. She wanted things her way and was known to throw a tantrum or two; she wore a T-shirt that read THE BOSS. The nannies had a tough time getting her to behave. They tried all sorts of punishments, some of which were overbearing. Consequently I assumed the role of protector in a household where it was easy to feel unprotected. There was a great distance between our rooms and our parents'—they slept at one end, we slept at the other. When a nanny told Hana the boogieman was going to get her, Hana ran to my room. When she became afraid of the dark, I went to her room and stayed the night. When our nannies punished her for breaking their rules, I defended her. My instinct was to stick up for my sister— and my mother as well. I was always assertive.

When I look back at my bedroom in Fremont Place, the picture is strange. It wasn't your average kid's room. It was set up for me, like a model home set up for potential buyers. It had an unlived-in feeling. It was almost too stunning, too perfect. The room was painted storybook yellow. Next to my daybed stood a stuffed baby deer, a real animal with bright eyes and shiny coat. I don't know who put it there, but it remained a fixture of my childhood. My door was half glass with a stained-glass rainbow, so anyone could peer in. A glass cabinet containing a collection of plates with images of fairies stood next to my bed. I found myself cleaning and organizing those plates until late in the night. I didn't play with many toys or dolls. Like the plates behind glass, I felt like I was living under glass. With so many strangers moving through the house, I felt on display; I felt vulnerable.

Two recurring dreams marked my early years in my father's mansion. In the first, the mansion becomes a maze where a killer is looking for me. I frantically run through the maze and crawl under a table. I somehow hang on to the table from below so the madman won't know I'm there. In the second dream, I'm called into Dad's study and told to sit on the lap of a woman who, just like that, turns into a skeleton. I run to the second floor, where a Mardi Gras scene is in full force, parties in every room, costumes, masks, devils, and dwarfs. I dash downstairs, out the front door, onto the porch where I'm met with thunder and lightning. A monsoon is washing over the mansion. The porch becomes a ship. Everyone aboard the ship is a skeleton. I run back inside, where everyone I touch turns into a skeleton. I'm trapped in the house with no one to protect me.

Did I feel unprotected? The fact that I was molested when I was five added to the weirdness I associate with that mansion. It happened on the third floor where my father housed his many trophies, a pool table, and a big-screen TV. I was molested by a relative who was six years older. The incident involved fondling that didn't last long. I put a quick stop to it. But I was left repulsed and confused. I was also left with the feeling that I never wanted to be touched by anyone. I withdrew even more.

For years I told no one, and of course that didn't help. I believe we need to get these secrets out there so they're no longer secrets. When they're secrets, they can choke you to death. When they're exposed, you can breathe. Now I know it's a common occurrence among families of every kind. Parents are instructed to discuss such disturbances with their kids, to let them process the feelings and express the hurt. My parents didn't have a clue. And neither did I. I didn't know what to do with the creepy feelings crawling over me. The experience left me with that awful knowledge that I had a secret. Such a secret is heavy on a child, resulting in an onrush of embarrassment and shame.

The great bulk of our supervision came from our nannies. Some were strict, some weren't. An Englishwoman, who was especially kind, was fired because my father's Muslim brothers felt he should employ blacks exclusively. Her dismissal pained me. She and I had become close; I had grown to trust and even love her. In that enormous house filled with strangers, connecting to a caring soul was important. When the connection was broken, I felt betrayed. In my childhood, people were always coming and going. I learned not to grow close to anyone.

Another nanny was a heavy drinker and had to be fired by Mom. The nanny didn't take it well. I stood there as she called me and Hana bastards. Just like that, my mother suddenly grabbed the woman by her blouse, yanked her up off her feet, and slammed her against the wall, seething, *"How dare you call my daughters names!"* We never heard from the nanny again.

Hana and I were shocked. We'd always seen Mom as gentle and demure. Now right before our eyes she stepped out of character, transforming herself into a warrior. I liked what I saw; it made me feel Mom really had my back.

Downstairs, Dad entertained a string of famous visitors. You might see Stevie Wonder, Michael Jackson, or John Travolta walking through the door. I saw how celebrities enjoyed one another's company, but I wasn't drawn to my father's famous friends. I was drawn instead to another black family who lived down the street. Those kids had a mom who was a housewife and a dad who was a physician. They ate together every night. Unlike us, there was a family room where everyone sat around and watched TV. The parents gave the kids rules and made sure they were obeyed. All this made me envious. I longed for such a family. At Christmas, when the whole family decorated the magnificent tree that sat in the center of their living room, I wished my family could do the same. I knew we couldn't.

Obviously Muslims don't celebrate Christmas. But because my father didn't like to see us sad, he said we could have a tree upstairs—as long as no one saw it. Mom, Hana, and I celebrated alone in semisecret. In our household, Christmas was far from a joyous season of family togetherness.

Hana's devotion to Dad was absolute. I was neutral. When he went away on trips, Hana cried till he returned. I never shed a tear. When he returned, he'd sometimes bring us along when he visited his friend Lonnie in her Westwood apartment. Lonnie had grown up across the street from my dad in Louisville, Kentucky. He had been her baby-sitter. When she came out to L.A. to go to UCLA, Dad paid for her education and expenses. We liked Lonnie. She was a smart lady, a little younger than my mom, with strong energy. At times Dad would take us over there when Lonnie was out. She knew he loved sweets and made sure there were plenty. I remember her telling us, "I know whenever you guys have been here because the cookie jar is empty and cookie crumbs are everywhere."

At the time, I didn't know anything was wrong. It took me

years to realize the inappropriateness of a married man introducing his kids to a special friend like Lonnie.

But neither my father nor mother had taken lessons in parenthood. They were stumbling in the dark, trying to make sense of their own lives, doing the best they could. Now I see what I couldn't see as a child:

Parents have complicated lives; like all human beings, they make mistakes.

Being with Dad, though, you knew the world saw him as more than a human being. He was viewed as a prophet. Eating in a restaurant or walking through a park with him, I'd hear someone screaming, "There's Ali!"

Being out with Mom, shopping for clothes or sitting in the doctor's office, I'd hear, "That's Ali's wife!" People were stunned by her presence.

The world embraced my parents' image. They clung to that image as long as they could. Neither wanted to look bad. But Mom simply got to the point where she had to move on. She decided to leave—and divorce—my father. Their long live-in separation no longer made sense. He hadn't been faithful, and she hadn't been able to play the part of subservient Muslim wife. She simply tired of the whole mess. Both proud people, they went their own ways. I didn't blame either one and I still don't.

I now recognize the courage it took for my mother to stand on her own.

When the final split came, though, I had no understanding of any of this. What nine-year-old does? All I knew is that Mom, Hana, and I were moving to another house.

Hana's heart was broken. Dad was her world. My heart was with my mom. As long as she was by my side, my world was intact.

COPING

WITH

CONFUSION

Before my mother took me and my sister and moved out of the mansion in Fremont Place, we were frequently visited by our brother and sisters. I was not close to my step-siblings, although later in life my sister Miya and I became friends. As you might expect, some of them had attitudes about my mom, whom they (or their mothers) blamed for breaking up their families. The truth is that Dad clung to the idea of family. Yet for all his gentle sweetness and love of children, he couldn't make us all come together as one big happy family. When all the kids got together, everyone fought to be his favorite; I could feel the jealousy in the air. As the youngest child, I was never comfortable with the group. When I heard nasty comments about my mom, I wanted to attack back. I didn't mind when my step-siblings went home.

I also didn't mind when my parents broke up for good. Besides, I had no love for the mansion. It was too big, too cold, too fancy. A smaller house brought the promise of a closer family, maybe even warmth and togetherness. So when we moved only a few blocks away on Longwood Avenue, I was happy. Besides getting to live in a cozier house, I'd get to have a cat. I named her Madonna. (Madonna and Whitney Houston were my two favorite singers.)

Cats became an important part of my life—and still are. I relate to cats. They're a little standoffish, never smother you with affection, yet thrive on affection. I love their mysteriously silent ways, their grace and independence. I longed for a normal family, and the idea of a cuddly little kitten seemed to bring that possibility a little closer.

That possibility was an illusion. It is for most of us. The idea of a normal family comes from TV, a Brady bunch of happy-go-lucky brothers and sisters whose silly little problems are solved in a half hour, Mom and Dad standing by with ear-to-ear smiles. Or *The Cosby Show*, where Daddy's a doctor, Mommy's a lawyer, and both are home all the time, their chief concern their children's progress in school.

I didn't do particularly well at school. I kept changing schools because I felt none suited me. I went to private schools, public schools, even a French-language school. In fact, I went to a half-dozen schools between kindergarten and sixth grade.

I was something of a fighter—
not an instigator but a defender of the smaller kids when they were bullied.

I wasn't the most obedient child. Teachers didn't intimidate me. Sometimes I had it easier because I was Ali's daughter, but sometimes I had it harder. Some teachers had to prove they wouldn't favor me—and went overboard. One time a teacher decided to punish me for talking during class. The punishment was to force me to hop like a frog. I flat-out refused. I thought it was stupid. I didn't mind standing in the corner, but I wasn't going to be humiliated by imitating a toad. The teacher became incensed, insisted, and finally, out of frustration, sent me to the office. I strutted out of the classroom proudly, saying, "I'm not hopping for anyone."

When it came to my schoolwork, my parents were preoccupied and paid little attention. At Le Lycée Français, for example, I told a teacher I was a third grader when, in truth, I was in second grade. Mom didn't even know I had been switched until the end of the year. By then I wanted out of the school anyway. I hated the uniforms and snobby attitudes. I'd never be comfortable in private schools. I wanted to mix it up with regular kids from regular families.

It was at the Third Street public school that I met my first true friend. I'll call her Alice. (To protect their privacy, I'm changing the names of all my friends in this book.) When I first met Alice, I was a little like my cat.

I was standoffish. And I also had some misguided racial attitudes. I remember telling Alice, who was black, that I was half white, because my mom had light skin. It was also important for me to let Alice know that my parents were rich. But fortunately Alice saw through my stupidity and liked me anyway. I liked the way she was relaxed in my company. She knew I was the daughter of a famous man—everyone knew—but didn't care. We could laugh and gossip and have fun like other kids. She invited me to her apartment in a middle-class neighborhood where she lived with her mother, a schoolteacher, and older brother. I immediately felt comfortable, as though I'd known these people my whole life. I felt like I belonged.

I enjoyed the freedom of being outside my gated community. It was a treat to be able to cross the street and go to Burger King. Going to the laundromat and folding sheets was fun. The idea of a family, even a fatherless family, busy with everyday tasks seemed absolutely wonderful. My own family couldn't provide me with such comforts, but Alice's family filled that void.

Meanwhile I saw how kids can be ignorant and cruel. At times I was both. I don't like admitting it, but my first months in public school brought out my prejudices. I'm glad they were brought out early. That gave me time to realize how my thinking was messed up.

I remember Norma. She was overweight and unattractive and picked on my sister Hana, who had a tough veneer. I was certain Hana could take care of herself. One day Norma instigated a fight with Hana. I watched in shock: The fight was over before it started. Hana didn't defend herself, and I felt bad there wasn't even time to jump in and fight for my sister. Suddenly my whole view of Hana changed. I realized I was the stronger of the two of us.

Next time I saw Norma, I gave her a piece of my mind. "You ain't nothing but ghetto," I told her.

"You don't even know what a ghetto is," Norma barked back.

"Yes I do."

"Then what is it?"

"A ghetto is where poor people run around barefoot."

Norma sneered. I thought she was going to try to fight me. She just laughed, though, and walked away. But in her little laugh I heard her hurt. And that made me feel bad.

The truth is that I didn't know the first thing about the ghetto. It was simply a way to say I'm superior to you.

My racial perspective was cockeyed.

I always had black friends, but they were other privileged kids who lived in or around Fremont Place. I had yet to discover the wide world of black Los Angeles. I harbored a bias, based on nothing but stupidity, and, instead of hitting Norma with my fists, I used words to wound her. As the school year went on, I felt remorse. I saw that Norma was okay, a girl who had family problems that made her angry and ready to fight. We never became friends, but I never insulted her again.

My two little fights in elementary school both involved boys. One spit on me, and, without thinking, I threw him down on the ground and kicked his butt. Another boy was beating up on someone smaller. The predator was about my size, so I figured it was a fair fight. We slugged it out. I landed enough blows where he never fooled with me again. Early on, I never backed away from fights. My mother was always trying to get me to avoid confrontations, arguing that was beneath me.

I'd tell Mom, "Look, I don't mind getting in the dirt when someone messes with me. Because when it's over, I can get back up, dust myself off, and move on."

I also grew increasingly interested in strength. I was dead

set on walking our two big Dobermans, Sheba and Samson, all by myself. With no man in the house, I saw someone needed to be strong—and that someone had to be me.

There was also a sweet side to my personality that masked the anger boiling up inside. As time went on, the anger intensified. Though I was obviously much closer to my mother than my father, that anger was principally directed against her. Mom was part of my daily life; Dad wasn't.

Dad became a distant figure. After Mom divorced him, he married Lonnie and moved to a big farm in rural Michigan. Physically and emotionally, he became more remote. It was a difficult time for him. In the mid-eighties, his physical deterioration was obvious to all. I remember a schoolmate taunting me with, "Your father's brain damaged! Your father's messed up!" I wanted to kick the kid in his mouth, but underneath I was more confused than angry. What *was* wrong with my dad? His condition was never discussed in full detail—not by him or Lonnie or my mom. We weren't told much at all. What we saw, though, couldn't be denied. His hands began to shake; his speech slurred. A change, which had begun when we were still small, was now evident in his every movement. The bigger change, though, was that he had left Los Angeles—and the glamorous life in his Fremont Place mansion—for a remote farm. Why? I never knew.

In the summers we'd usually visit him and Lonnie in Michigan. When we were there, he'd forget my age. That had nothing to do with his condition. Dad always had trouble remembering basic facts about all his kids. The only reason he may have remembered me clearly was because, of all his children, I was the one who refused to be a Muslim. I refused to go the mosque, refused to pray five times a day, refused to pretend that the religion held any interest for me. I respected my father's devotion—I still do—but devotion isn't anything I can fake. When spirituality came, it came by way of my mother, not my father. And that wouldn't be for years.

At this delicate time in my life—ages eight through ten—my parents were undergoing drastic changes in their own lives. They were each struggling to redefine themselves—he as a former champ, she as a former wife. Naturally I didn't have a clue, only that they were both distancing themselves from their children. Because my mother had physical custody of us, a point never contested by Dad, she became my world. We forged a bond that was tested and tormented, but never broken.

I lacked the respect for my mother that I now have. She was the object of barbs and nasty stories; she was the woman who wouldn't conform to the champ and found the guts to go her own way. She traveled a lonely road. After the divorce, she went through the heaviest drama of her life. The drama rolled over to her daughters.

This is my book, not my mother's. One day she'll write her own. Rather than trample on her story, I wish to stay on mine. But because our lives are intricately intertwined, there's no way to tell one story without touching on the other. I don't want to judge anyone, least of all my mother. I also believe in discretion and I respect her privacy. To tell you what happened to me, though, I'm going to have to tell you what happened to Mom—at least from my point of view.

Veronica Porche is a proud woman. Understandably so. She has a variety of talents and interests. After the divorce, *Good Morning, America* approached her about being an on-the-air host in New York. She turned down the offer because she didn't want to live there. She wanted to concentrate on interior decoration. As I've said, appearances are important to my mother, just as they are to my dad. There were times when she asked us to call her "Veronica" in public. "You girls look much older than you are," she explained, "and calling me 'Mom' will make people think I'm older than I am."

When my mother leaves the house, for whatever occasion, everything about her is in order—hair, dress, shoes. She speaks in a quietly refined voice and uses perfect English. She has impeccable manners and is expert at avoiding confrontations. For all the underground discord, I never saw a single confrontation between her and Dad. She is exceedingly guarded and scrupulously private. So you can imagine how disturbing it was to watch her, the most composed of ladies, go through her drama. I wasn't ready for any of it.

Mom bought a house on Windsor Boulevard in Hancock Park, a stately neighborhood adjacent to Fremont Place. She spent months decorating before we moved in. Less than a mansion, it was a grand house on an acre of land—four bedrooms, three baths, study, large living room, formal dining room, breakfast room, housekeeper's quarters. Mom was busy at design school, and the house reflected her exquisite taste. My room was pink. Even the wallpaper had borders of little pink ribbons.

I liked feminine colors and soft feminine furniture. By age ten, I cared about my appearance. I was considered tall and grew confident in my height. Only once can I remember slouching at school for a boy who was shorter and especially cute. Ten is also the age when I got my first period. It all went well. Mom had told me what to expect. Mom was extremely conscientious that way. She had also given me a children's book on sex education that spelled out the facts.

At age ten or eleven I was molested again, this time by a member of my mother's family. He was a man in his late twenties. One time he came into my room at night—this is when we lived on Windsor—and rubbed my leg. I didn't know what to do, so I did nothing. I'd guess most kids do nothing. You stay there and hope he goes away. You hope it's not really happening. But it was. Several times he tried to kiss me. Once when he and I were alone, he slipped in a porn tape and exposed his penis. At that point I found the courage to run from the room and finally tell my mother. It took Mom years to believe it. That, too, must be a common pattern. What adult wants to believe her relative is harming her child? You'd rather believe the kid's overactive imagination has been stimulated by too many movies or TV shows.

But molestation really happens.

Now that I'm older, I know molestation is frighteningly common.

Back then I thought it was just me. I know that I wanted my fright to be made all right by my mother. I wanted her to rescue me, hold me, tell me that yes, she knows how awful and creepy it must have been. It maddened me to see my experience dismissed. How do you calculate the damage? All I know is that even today I don't liked being touched, even innocently, by people I don't know. I wish my mother and I could have dealt with the situation and given it closure.

Mothers and daughters, dancing around each other, looking for ways to relate, missing the signals, getting all entangled.

The dance goes on and on.

The dance between my mother and me started disintegrating into angry discord when we moved to Windsor. That's when my mom got into a new relationship.

Mom's boyfriend was attractive, a so-called musician. I'll call him Walter. He seemed to be nice and quite successful. He acted like he had it together. Once we got to know him better, though, he turned out to have nothing—only the ability to charm my mother. Charm is probably too weak a word. To my mind, he controlled and manipulated her. He took over her life and tried to take over ours. It took me a few months to see through his facade, but by then he had moved into our house on Windsor. I resented the hell out of that. I saw him as an intrusion. I was all over Mom, telling her that she was jumping too quickly into another relationship. I was talking like *I* was the mother.

Tension mounted. Walter didn't like me any more than I liked him. Then one afternoon he called us all into the breakfast room. By then he'd been living in our house for a couple of months. Gradually he'd been dominating my mother's life. She was no longer in design school. Seemed like she was living only to make this man happy.

"I've called you together to have a family meeting," he announced.

What family? I thought to myself. *You're not family.*

As he spoke he held a wooden paddle in his hand. *What's up with that? How could my mother permit this man to threaten us with a paddle?*

"There's going to be some changes around here," he went on. "Now that I'm the man of the house."

I couldn't hold my tongue. I had to say it. "Who the hell do you think you are?"

COPING WITH CONFUSION

Mom was seated at the table, slouched, her eyes looking down. To me, she looked defeated. Hana was standing. She looked frightened. She said, "Quiet, Laila, just be quiet."

"You're going to show some respect," Walter insisted, playing with the paddle.

"You gonna hit me with that thing?" I said. "Is that what you intend to do?"

He got up and approached me. I walked right over to him, stuck my face an inch away from his and said it plainly. "You hit me with that thing and I'll hit you back."

"Laila!" Mom protested. There were tears in her eyes.

"You'll learn respect," said Walter. "Especially when we move to Malibu."

"Move to Malibu? Who's moving to Malibu?"

"We are," Walter went on. "We're selling this house and buying a place in Malibu."

"We? I'm not going anywhere!"

"The hell you're not."

I didn't believe him. "Mom just got through decorating this place. It's all fixed up. Mom's never even mentioned Malibu."

Mom kept her eyes down. Finally she said, "We'll discuss all this later, Laila."

"I want to know right now," I insisted. "I want to know that we're not moving to Malibu."

"You'll do what I say," said Walter.

"You're an asshole!" I said the words. Mama was horrified; Hana was horrified; Walter was shocked. I saw his fingers tight-

en on the grip of the paddle. I knew he wanted to hit me, but something in my eyes kept him away.

"Doesn't matter what you say," Walter smirked. "You ain't nothing but a kid with a smart mouth. Like it or not, we're moving to Malibu."

DEALING
WITH
DYSFUNCTION

People spend their lives saving their money to move to Malibu. They long to live at the beach away from the crowded city. In the canyons and the hills, multimillionaires build dream castles. The weather's ideal, the air is fresh, and the sunsets are glorious.

So why didn't I like it? What was wrong with me?

I couldn't relate to anyone or anything. All I knew was that I was being dragged away from my friends in L.A., from the childhood neighborhoods I knew and liked. I remember the first time we drove out there.

Cozy and warm, Mom and Walter are sitting in the front seat of the Jeep with the heat blasting. Hana and I are in the back with the top down and the wind blowing in our faces. We're rolling up Pacific Coast Highway, growing colder by the minute. Mom and Walter are talking, but I can't hear a word they're saying. Mom keeps turning around and looking back; I can see in her eyes that she's concerned about us. The drive seems to go on forever. We drive through Santa Monica, past the old Getty Museum, even beyond Pepperdine University. Feels like we're driving to Alaska. An hour goes by before we turn off the highway and head into the Malibu hills. The road is twisted, the houses far apart, the landscape parched. We pull up in front of a big L-shaped house in the middle of nowhere. "The drive was worth it," says Walter. "It's beautiful," my mother agrees. I don't say a word.

The Malibu move happened when I was twelve. If I had been angry before, my anger now turned to fury. Mom was with a man I couldn't stand, someone whose macho ways provoked the fighting rebel inside me. Even worse, Mom was being controlled by this man. She was moving where he wanted to move, doing what he wanted done. It was bad enough to see her so subservient. But when her subservience implicated me, I was mad enough to curse her out. Neither Hana nor I were ever asked where we might want to live or what school we might want to attend. Walter wanted Malibu, so Malibu it was. And Mom thought that's what she wanted as well.

The roles got reversed. The script got flipped. I got to feeling like the protective mother. In my view, Mom was losing her grasp on reality; her strength was being sapped by the pressures of her postdivorce life. I saw it as weakness, and weakness in women infuriates me. Remember, I'm the little girl who had to walk our dogs Samson and Sheba, each of whom weighed more than me. It's clear to me now that little girls should stay little girls and mothers remain mothers.

Role reversals spin us out and make us crazy.

But back then I didn't have a clue. For years, Mom and I went a little crazy.

Making matters worse, the drastic move came at a time when I was comfortable with my life in L.A. Things had been going reasonably well. I had my friend Alice, who had become like a sister, and also my friend I'll call Tia.

If Alice was down to earth, Tia was out in space. She was always looking to have fun. Older than me, Tia went to private school and lived in my old L.A. neighborhood. Her parents spoiled her royally. She got a brand-new fire-engine red Porsche in the driveway the day she turned sixteen. Tia—or her Porsche—attracted all the fine young brothers. This was still innocent stuff—no sex involved—but things were changing.

Hormones were kicking in. The boys were looking, and we were looking back at them, with a smile. Our figures were taking shape. We just knew we were fine. There were several guys I considered cute but was never serious about any of them. I could float between Tia's scene in Hancock Park and Alice's life in mid-city and feel comfortable all the way around.

Malibu was the height of discomfort. I was stuck in the middle of nowhere. There were no nearby neighbors, nowhere to walk, nothing to do. You needed a navigator to find our house, a rambling structure whose layout only reinforced the separation between me and Mom. At first glance the home was pretty, a modern Spanish design, hand-painted tiles, off-white walls, earth tone modern furniture, an airy beach house nestled in the Malibu hills. The decor was lovely. The problem was the layout. The house was essentially cut in two. Mom and Walter lived in the main section, and Hana and I were cut off in quarters of our own.

The main house had a large kitchen, three bedrooms, a family area, and Walter's recording studio—plus a breathtaking view of the ocean a couple of miles down the mountainside. A glass door separated the main section from the guest quarters, where Hana and I lived. We had our own phone number and own entrance that led to a small kitchen, a sitting area, and, upstairs, two bedrooms and a bath. At first we liked the idea of living apart. We felt mature and happy to be away from Walter. But it soon became clear that Walter chose the house because of the floor plan. He wanted us out of sight so he could pretend we didn't exist. It wasn't long before he found an excuse to permanently lock the door that separated us from him and Mom. "I have valuable equipment in here," he said. *"The door stays locked at all times."*

DEALING WITH DYSFUNCTION

I was certain my mother would never allow us to be locked out. I was wrong. Walter had completely brainwashed her. He even persuaded her to forbid us to put up pictures of our father. I was stunned as she stood there and justified his action about the locked door. "He needs his privacy," she said, parroting his line. "He needs to protect his equipment." I knew she was just making excuses for him. I became furious, but because I hated him so much I didn't want to give him the satisfaction of seeing me enraged. So I pretended I didn't care.

That locked door became a symbol of everything wrong between me and Mom. I couldn't get past it. Communication was cut off. There were no family meals. Hana and I cooked our own dinner, ate by ourselves, and when we needed to talk to my mother, we called her on her separate line. I could have banged on the door until she heard me, but I had too much pride.

I watched Mom turn into another person. Walter had insomnia and kept her up all night. He abused her emotionally and acted like she was put on earth to serve him. As time went on, she ate less and less. She looked emaciated as she retreated deeper into a relationship none of us understood. This is when I lost respect for my mother, when my antagonism toward her grew ugly.

Meanwhile, living in Malibu gave me my first taste of **racism.**

I felt unwelcome. People looked at us as though we didn't belong. Hana and I were enrolled in Malibu Park School. Aside from a very few blacks, the school was all white. I disliked standing out, yet that was the situation: I stood out because I was black and because I was Muhammad Ali's daughter.

The kids were stuck-up and sheltered. Hana and I were popular, I believe, because of our father and also because we were leaders, not followers. We were more confident and mature than our schoolmates who, from time to time, invited us to their parties. But when we saw kids doing drugs and having sex in the bushes, we got out of there in a hurry. Their definition of fun was different than ours.

Malibu turned my whole world upside down. I didn't like home and I didn't like school. The plain truth was that I didn't like life.

The bus schedule became my best friend. A couple of months at Malibu Park and I began thinking of ways to get away. Rather than moan and groan about how I hated my existence, I was looking to change it as soon as I could. The first—and easiest—change meant catching the bus. It was a long walk down the hill, but worth it. The buses were far and few between, and it took over an hour to get to L.A.—when traffic was bad, ninety minutes—but I didn't care. I was willing to sit on that bus and watch the world go by, willing to do anything to get out of the house and see my friends in the city.

I rode the bus weekend after weekend. I watched the waves and the surfers, the tourists and the beach bums; I sighed as we crept along bumper to bumper; I studied the cloudless sky; I grew restless until we finally arrived in Santa Monica and headed east. By the time I got out in the mid-Wilshire district, Malibu had left my mind. Whether Tia or Alice, my friends were my escape and entertainment. Their families became my family.

My father was family, but his life on the Michigan farm had little to do with me. He'd invite us for summer visits. On one of those visits I decided to get a job at McDonald's. Some people thought it was crazy for Ali's daughter to work in a fast-food restaurant, but I didn't care what they thought. I wanted to make money and be independent. Dad accepted my decision and, in fact, used it as an excuse to drop by for apple pie and ice cream.

I was close enough to my father to express my concern about Mom—that she was growing remote, losing weight, looking distressed. I poured out my heart, saying that I thought Walter was evil and taking our mom away from us. Dad listened carefully and then cried. He's always had a special place in his heart for my mother. He knew she was just a baby when he met her and realized he could have treated her better. It pained him to learn that she was having a hard time with another man. His tears touched me. I've always been touched by my father's sweetness. Yet even though he felt bad, he didn't offer advice or help. His life was changing as well. Lonnie was playing an increasingly larger role, making all the business decisions, while Dad devoted himself to Islam and humanitarian work.

When Mom learned I had mentioned her personal situation to my father, she grew angry and accused me of broadcasting her business. I could see she was ashamed, which is why she wanted to keep it all secret.

Meanwhile, my schoolwork was failing. No one really noticed—Dad was too far away physically and Mom too far away emotionally. Mom was lost behind that locked door. My intolerance intensified. When Walter made a rare appearance, I offered him nothing but contempt. His fury grew. Although he never hit me, he ordered Mom to do so. She didn't have the heart, but she also lacked the strength to defy him. Her solution was to come over to our side of the house and ask me to fake it. "Scream," she whispered, "while I hit the bed. He'll think I'm doing what he wants." I went along with the sad charade. It was so sad, in fact, that when it was over, Mom and I were both crying.

I missed school so often that the truant officer came around to our house. It was ten in the morning, and I was putting away groceries.

"Why are you doing housework?" she asked. "You're sup-posed to be in school. Is your mother home?"

"Yes," I said, seeing Mom's car in the driveway. "Go to the other door." I pointed out Mom's separate section of the house. I was always ashamed of our separate quarters and tried to hide it.

"I want to talk to her."

She knocked on the door repeatedly, but no one answered. We called her on the phone, but no one picked up.

"Where *is* your mother?" the officer wanted to know.

I wanted to know the same thing. The whole episode left me embarrassed.

The whole year at school was strained. I felt deeply alone. The one connection I did make was with a woman who worked in the school office whom I'll call Miss Mary. Miss Mary had a clerical job behind a desk. She read the trouble in my eyes and sensed my need for guidance. The first time she reached out to me I was waiting on the steps in front of school. Once again Mom hadn't shown up and I was ready to walk home.

"Hey, Laila," said Miss Mary, "why don't you let me give you a ride?"

Miss Mary drove a raggedy pickup truck. She was a large white lady with an unkempt appearance and happy-go-lucky personality. She had a big shaggy dog and a seven-year-old daughter she was raising alone in a Malibu trailer park. Her truck and trailer smelled like her dog. Some might consider Miss Mary low class, but I didn't see her that way; I liked her the minute I met her. She listened to my problems, and we became friends. Miss Mary was one of the first real listeners I'd ever met. When most people listen, you sense how they can't wait for you to stop talking so they can start. Most people listen with half an ear. Miss Mary listened with her whole heart. Best of all, when I was through talking she didn't try to tell me what to do. She didn't offer easy answers or "coulds" or "shoulds." She simply listened. I knew she liked me for me and had my best interests at heart. I also knew I could trust her with my most personal feelings. Miss Mary's trailer became my refuge. Miss Mary loved me, and so did her little daughter.

It was a critical time in my life, and to feel loved, unconditionally loved, made all the difference in the world.

Miss Mary was real. She liked her Jack Daniel's; her language was straightforward. But she didn't say anything she didn't mean.

I loved hanging out in her little kitchen and learning how to make vegetable soup. In Malibu, where million-dollar houses are the norm, I was happy in a trailer. I was relaxed riding around in her funky pickup; I enjoyed watching a mother easily and naturally communicate with a daughter. Miss Mary made Malibu a little easier.

By the seventh grade—my second year at Malibu Park—I was spending more and more time in L.A. With my thick brown glasses, I looked a little nerdy but I still thought I was cute. At thirteen and fourteen, I was socializing with kids eighteen and nineteen. I still longed to be older than I was. I swore to my mom that the minute I turned eighteen, I would move out, attend college, and support myself by doing nails. I still dreamed of driving my own car. Short of that, I found ways to steal Mom's Jeep.

You could look at it two ways—either I was manipulative or Mom was easily manipulated. It was probably both. Anyway, I'd lie and say that a friend with a license would be driving, not me. Mom refused, but my begging was so unrelenting and obnoxious that she finally caved. I'd pick a time she was out with Walter and then drive off myself. Without a license, much less driving lessons, I'd peel off and speed down the curvy coastline to L.A.

This was a time in my life when much older men—some twenty-five, some thirty—were approaching me. Wearing tight jeans, I was aware of my figure. All girls are. I couldn't help but be a little flattered when the guys noticed. But I was honest. I'd tell them, "Look, I'm only fourteen."

Some would reply, "Never mind."

Others would say, "So?" and pursue the matter further.

Finally, though, I had no interest in strange men. I strongly declined all such invitations. My social life centered on hanging out with Alice and Tia. I was comfortable with black friends and white friends and all colors in between. We went to parties, mostly in people's houses, not clubs. We listened to rap and r&b. Like most kids, we hung out in the malls, walking in groups, looking in store windows, shopping, and, of course, checking the boys who were checking us. It was at one such mall—the Westside Pavilion—where I met a friend I'll call Mike, the first love of my life. My life was about to change in big ways.

EXERCISING

RESTRAINT

n Saturday afternoon the Westside Pavilion was the place to be. Wall-to-wall teens, cruising past the Gap, sampling new CDs, the shoe stores, the department stores, checking out the scene.

Me and my girls were walking one way; Mike and his friends were walking the other.

I'd seen him around. I'd noticed his laid-back manner. He was cute, a little taller than me, with light brown coloring and an easy smile. He had a football build, not perfect but solid— and big brown eyes. His hair was short and neat. He was a good dresser and wore cologne that smelled fresh.

When our groups converged, we stopped to talk. Mike came over to me.

"How are you doing?" he asked.

Meeting men—meeting anyone—I've never been one to overreact. I'm reserved. "I'm fine," I said.

"You live around here?" Mike wanted to know.

"Actually out in Malibu."

"Wow. That's quite a trip."

I had to smile. "You don't know the half of it."

As we paired off from the group and walked around the mall, the conversation continued. We kept it light. Something about Mike felt right. He wasn't pushing it. He wasn't hitting on me. He was a little shy himself, and his words were genuine. When he ran out of things to say, he kept quiet. He wasn't afraid of silence. I wasn't easily impressed by guys, yet Mike caught my attention because he didn't try to impress me. I didn't like giving out my number—I rarely did—but I gave it to Mike.

I thought about him that night and the next day. I thought about his beautiful smile. Mike was always smiling. I thought about how we were both Capricorns, strong-minded and stubborn. I thought about the sincerity of his questions. He really listened to me—the way Miss Mary listened—with care and concern.

He also expressed a sensitivity most guys lack.

He wasn't boastful or opinionated, didn't talk loud or long, wasn't trying to prove anything. He was himself, plain and simple. He said he would call me. Twenty-four hours later, he did what he said.

If my life had revolved around my L.A. weekends before, now it was doubly true. Mike lived just off Washington Boulevard, a few blocks from where Marvin Gaye had lived and died, in the predominantly black Crenshaw district of L.A. Mike and his mom, a schoolteacher, shared an apartment that soon became my home away from home. Mike's mom was an intelligent and strong black woman who treated me like family. Mike was three years older than me. Emotionally, though, we were on the same level. We really enjoyed each other's company. He wasn't a bullshitter, and neither was I.

I lived for the weekends when I got to see Mike. There were times when he found a ride or took the bus to Malibu. Mostly, though, we were at his apartment back in L.A. My sister Hana didn't understand. All the time I was going with Mike, she called me a hootchie mama. She thought I could do better than him. She didn't realize that Mike was good for me; she didn't see how he let me be me. I could relax around him and his mom and enjoy the closeness of their relationship.

Out on Washington Boulevard, I'd hear the crack of gunfire. Folks talked about drive-bys that happened on their street. Mike had neighbors his age, identical twins I'll call Tom and Tim. Tom was an honor student at Dorsey High, where Mike went to school. Tim was a Blood. They both were well mannered and sweet. If Mike hadn't told me, I couldn't tell you which was the good boy and which was the gang banger.

I wasn't completely honest with Mike's mom. I represented myself as older than I was. If you didn't know, you'd think I was seventeen, not fourteen. Fourteen seemed too young to have a serious boyfriend. But fourteen was the age when I lost my virginity. It happened in the apartment when Mike's mom was off teaching school.

I did not exercise sexual restraint. Truth is, I didn't come close to exercising restraint. I didn't even have any conflicts about it. The issue—*do I or don't I?*—was something I never would have discussed with my dad in a million years, even if we had been closer. Mom was off in her own world, and my anger at her—for staying with Walter—was so strong I couldn't talk to her without losing my temper.

Why did I consent to sex at so young an age? Part of it was curiosity. I'd heard about it; now I wanted to see what it was. I was also sure I was in love. It wasn't a matter of desire; and it wasn't because Mike was pressuring me. He wasn't that kind of guy.

Then why didn't I have better sense? Maybe it was lack of self-esteem typical of most young girls. We aren't secure enough to say no. We haven't learned how to protect ourselves from emotional and physical harm. And many of us don't have the advantage of parental guidance.

At fourteen—
or even younger—
every daughter needs
the "don't give it up"
speech.

Here's my version of that speech for any young girl who can relate to my story: If you think you're ready, think again. You're not. I thought I was ready and I was dead wrong. I needed someone to tell me—emphatically—to wait until I was grown, until I was out of the house and responsible for myself. Life is confusing enough when you're still living at home. Adding to that confusion by engaging in early sex is crazy. Not to mention harmful—and dangerous.

Physically, my first experience was no revelation. We didn't make love; we had sex. It would take me years to learn the true nature of lovemaking. I just fell into it. It was a mistake, but at the time you couldn't have told me.

You couldn't have told me because you wouldn't have known. I didn't tell a soul—not Tia, not Alice, not Hana, and not Mom. Mike used condoms, so I thought I was safe, but the dangers never left my mind entirely. What if the condom broke?

(One time it did.) What about those transmitted diseases? What about AIDS? What about getting pregnant? The fears outweighed the pleasures.

My main pleasure was having a friend, not having sex. What I didn't know then—what most young females don't know—is the huge emotional distance between teen girls and teen boys. They're in one place and we're in another. We're looking for romantic attachment and security; they're looking for sex. Ninety-five percent of the guys have no sense of loyalty. It's not part of their makeup. They're looking to score, score, score. Their hormones are raging ahead of ours; and it's their hormones, not their heads, driving them on.

The young girls I knew having sex wanted to be liked. That was their main motivation. *If I let this guy, he'll like me. He'll spend all his time with me.* That's a sad commentary on our lack of self-respect. In my own case, I lacked clarity. I didn't know about proper boundaries. To enforce those boundaries would have taken a different person. I was too caught up in escaping my mother's house to have healthy ideas about my own behavior. I was dead set on doing what I wanted to do. Having sex, inappropriate and foolish as it was, seemed perfectly okay.

Meanwhile, my relationship with my mother deteriorated. I'm remorseful about the things I said. Seeing her suffer in this sick relationship with Walter, I grew incensed. I saw her as stupid and weak; I couldn't appreciate her emotional struggles. She was going through the necessary changes to become the woman she is today, but I didn't see that. All I saw was how

Walter controlled her. When I thought she was trying to control me, I snapped.

It's ugly when a child curses a parent, but that's just what I was doing. One time in the kitchen when I bad-mouthed Walter, Mom slapped me. That convinced me that she put him above me. I became furious and lashed out. "Bitch," I snarled, "do that again and I'll fuck you up!"

Mom gasped. Hana grabbed me, afraid I was about to attack our mother. I wasn't. No matter how crazy my rage, I could never hurt my mother—at least not physically.

I was hurt because I felt rejected. I loved my mother so much I had to know she loved me back. In my young mind, though, her actions said all she cared about was Walter. I took all my hurt feelings and dumped them on her. Daughters dump on mothers because they know mothers will take it. It's a safe place to do the dumping. That doesn't make it fair, just understandable. I wish I had understood my mental condition more; I wish I could have stopped myself and avoided the terrible scenes. Given her own problems, the last thing in the world Mom needed was her baby daughter turning against her.

My only hope was to escape—escape to Mike's house or to Tia's or Alice's. Desperate to spend more time in L.A. and be close to my friends, I came up with a plan. There was a school close to Alice's house that interested me, Los Angeles Center for Enriched Studies (LACES), an arts-oriented school around Venice Boulevard and Fairfax. They accepted out-of-town applicants. On my own, I applied for eighth grade admission. My grades at Malibu Park were below average, but being Ali's daughter was enough to get me in. Even though I was sorry that Alice didn't get in, I accepted the preferential treatment—anything to get out of Malibu Park school. Going to LACES, I'd be even more of a slave to the city bus system, but I didn't care.

My mother didn't argue. She saw I'd done my research and had my act together. Strange, but even in the midst of my angriest moments I was self-sufficient. If I wanted something, I'd find a way to get it.

I was determined to change my life— then and now.

The summer before eighth grade was especially enjoyable for me. Only one evening gave me pause for thought.

I went to a party with my girls. Everyone was hanging out, talking, dancing. I was in the living room with Tia when I noticed Mike deep in conversation with a girl in the kitchen. She seemed interested in his every word. Her most noticeable features were her prominent breasts, which she put on display, shoulders back, chest thrust forward. A wave of jealousy washed over me.

"Who's that girl?" I asked Tia.

Next thing I knew Miss Thing had vanished and Mike was by my side. I decided not to say a word. I sensed Mike was uneasy. Something wasn't right, but I left it alone. We went back to his place. I forgot the girl. It was one of those balmy August nights when the world seemed sweet and filled with promise. I started talking about the new school year; I was excited about transferring.

"I've been thinking about that," said Mike. "I don't think it's a good idea."

"Where's that coming from?" I wanted to know.

"I think you'll be happier staying in Malibu."

"What are you taking about, Mike? I hate Malibu."

"But school is different around here. It's not for you."

"Why?"

"It's just different."

"How?"

"The people are rougher."

"And I won't be able to take it?"

"I'm telling you, Laila, you're better off staying put."

Mike had a point—but I didn't quite get it. Not yet anyway.

Misty Malibu morning. The ocean fog covered our house and the surrounding hills. I was up early. I picked out my clothes carefully—Guess? jeans, new top, spotless white tennis shoes.

It was a big day, my first at LACES, and I was eager to get there. I made it down to the bus stop with ten minutes to spare. Out of the fog, the bus rolled in and I was on my way. New school, new kids, new life. I was certain eighth grade would be my best year ever. This was the change I needed.

No transfer student is comfortable the first day. I was no different. Butterflies fluttered inside my stomach. I went to homeroom, got my class assignments, and was on my way down the hallway when I suddenly stopped dead in my tracks. Coming toward me was Mike. That would be puzzling enough. Mike went to Dorsey High. What was he doing here? Making it doubly troublesome, though, was the girl on his arm. Miss Thing from the party. And making it triply troublesome was his snub. The second my eyes locked on his, he looked away. He completely ignored me.

I was devastated. I was also pissed at myself for not saying something. Why did I just let him walk by like that? Why didn't I yell out his name? The girl didn't recognize me. Maybe she hadn't seen me the night of the party. Maybe I was going crazy. Maybe it wasn't Mike. But of course it was Mike. He didn't have a twin. But he sure as hell was leading a double life.

I was out of it all day. I couldn't stop thinking about what I saw. I couldn't stop inventing scenarios. Later that afternoon, I spotted Mike in the hallway. He quickly walked over, looked around, and, seeing the coast was clear, gently kissed me the cheek.

"What the hell . . ." I started to say.

"I transferred here at the last minute."

"So why didn't you tell me?"

"This isn't the right time to talk."

"Who's that girl you were with?"

"Just an old friend."

"Looked like she was more than a friend."

"This isn't the time for us to talk."

"Fine. Then when *will* we talk?"

"Let's just chill for a while."

"Look, Mike, I don't get it."

And neither did he, because by the time those words were out of my mouth, the boy was up and gone.

When school was out, Mom came to pick me up. She figured I might have had a hard day. Driving up Pacific Coast Highway back to Malibu, there was silence between us. I needed to talk. My mother, unlike most, didn't ask a lot of questions. If I didn't bring up my private life, she'd never mention it. But this time I was so confused I had to open up. She listened sympathetically but gave no strong opinion about what I should do. At the same time, I got the feeling she expected me to break up with him. But how could I do that? How could I dump him if he had already dumped me? I was thoroughly humiliated.

It didn't take long to learn the name of the girl I'll call Dee Dee. She was a well-known cheerleader. Miss Thing thought she was all that. It was of little comfort to note that she had a flat butt and knock knees. Every time I turned the corner, there she was. And there was Mike, averting his eyes whenever I came into his field of vision.

For months I stuffed my hurt. My attitude was *the hell with both of them. If he wants her, let him have her.* Deep down, though, I was hurt. How could I have been such a fool? Mike was the nicest guy I'd ever met. Sweet. Considerate. Caring. He never manipulated or tried to control me. If you had asked me, I'd have vouched for his loyalty. Running around with another girl? Impossible. So when the shit hit the fan, I was floored. I had my first big dose of reality—and rejection.

I hated being played.

I felt silly and stupid and, worst of all, vulnerable.

After all, Mike was more than my boyfriend; he was my best friend. In my naive mind, that love was inviolable. He and I were joined, not simply in body but spirit. Neither one of us would dare break that bond. I just didn't see it coming. For all my certainty, I didn't have the foggiest notion about boys. My idealized notions about male/female relationships and romance came crashing down. When a young girl has sex with a boy, she does so—at least I did—with heartfelt sincerity. But to the guy it's no more serious than playing basketball. When the game's over, he starts looking for another game. And another.

And then another. If you're not willing to play again, he'll find someone who is.

Like a million girls before me, I suffered. I cried myself to sleep. I went to school seething with hurt and anger. It wasn't just Mike's betrayal that haunted me; it was his mom's as well. She had to know about Dee Dee. She had to know her son was mistreating two young ladies. How could she just stand around and smile? She'd been like a second mother to me. Why didn't she give me a hint? Why didn't she stop her son from living a lie? I also had wonder to myself, *who did she like better, me or Miss Thing?*

All these were rhetorical questions. As the school year went on, I never said anything. I grew more sullen. LACES was nothing like I thought it'd be. Everyone knew everyone's business. The boys were soft and the girls stuck-up. It was like a little private school, just the sort of ambience I disliked. The social scene was run by cliques. Dee Dee ran with the in-crowd. I hated thinking this way, but seeing Dee Dee in her element triggered my self-doubts. I worried that she was prettier than me, smarter, better in a lot of ways. As much as I tried to forget them, I couldn't help but notice when both Dee Dee and Mike were absent on the same day. I knew they were together. Rejected, infuriated, I lived with all this unspoken anger a long time. Finally, I couldn't take it anymore. I decided to take matters in my own hands. To hell with restraint. I was going read Miss Thing the riot act.

I made my move through a girl who was friendly with us both. I asked her to arrange for Dee Dee to meet me at Mc-

Donald's. Dee Dee agreed, and the next day we were sitting across from each under the golden arches. She munched on fries. I sipped a Coke. I kicked off the discussion.

"You should know that Mike and I were together for a year."

With a confused and pissed look, she said, "How can that be? He's been spending all his time with me."

I got specific. I named dates, people, and places—when we met, where we met, the address of his apartment. I revealed details about his mom only a close friend would know. I even mentioned the party where I had seen Dee Dee. She claimed not to have seen me.

I put it to her simply. "Look," I said, "he's been playing us both."

"He wasn't playing when he gave me this necklace." She took the gold chain off her neck and showed it to me. Then her pager went off.

"You see," she said. "That's him right now."

"All right," I conceded, "if you want to know the truth, ask Mike to meet you at your house. When he gets there, you and I will greet him together. Don't give him advance warning. Just check out the expression on his face. Then ask him—with me standing right there—what kind of relationship we had. Ask him whether we were together for over a year. Ask him whether I practically lived at his place with him and his mom. Just ask him."

Dee Dee turned her eyes from mine. As she wolfed down a couple of fries, I could hear the wheels turning in her head. She didn't know who—or what—to believe.

"Okay," she finally said. "Come over in an hour."

Perfect! This was the confrontation I'd been wanting. Even dreaming of. The moment of truth was at hand.

An hour later I showed up at Dee Dee's. She took me on a tour of her house. "This is the water bed," she said, "where me and Mike get down." My heart was racing as she overexplained and overshowed: "Me and Mike do this . . . me and Mike do that . . ." I couldn't quite believe I was in the house where Mike had betrayed me, talking to the girl he'd betrayed me with. I didn't want to be there, yet I was. Being at the scene of the crime was fascinating. I couldn't wait for Mike to show up and get busted. I wanted to see how Miss Thing was going to handle the truth.

My scenario never happened. Dee Dee flipped the script. Before Mike arrived, she had called him and told him what was up. She gave him time so, like a slick politician, he could prepare a statement. He told her he had merely kissed me—once. He said he barely knew me. So when he walked through the door, he was all calm. He could play off the confrontation like it was nothing. He acted like I was just some flighty girl with nothing better to do than invent a fantastic love story. "I believe Mike," Dee Dee said to me. "I believe every word he says."

For the rest of my days at LACES, life was miserable. Dee Dee and I became sworn enemies. She stayed with Mike and couldn't stop slandering my name. She told everyone that I was nothing more than a girl Mike had once screwed over. Meanwhile, she was his true love.

I saw myself as a nice person, but this mess was too much

for anyone to take. I plotted to kick Dee Dee's butt for disrespecting me, making me look bad, and slandering my name. I prided myself on having a good reputation, and now this fool was ruining it. I was ready to do serious damage, but Miss Thing ran at the mere mention of a confrontation; I never got my chance.

My only consolation was the failure of her romance with Mike. They were utterly miserable together. I was glad. All during ninth grade, I was delighted to see them fighting and finally breaking up. Mike eventually left LACES for another school. I was happy. I thought that would be the end of my chapter with Mike. I didn't know that an even more intense chapter was about to be written.

SEPARATING
RIGHT FROM
WRONG

Mom wouldn't talk about it, but her relationship with Walter had gone from bad to worse. Their locked door couldn't muffle the sounds of their arguments. Walter was always on edge, always yelling about something. Every day my mother looked more and more traumatized. He kept her up all night—his insomnia required her company—so during the day she was tired and cranky. He claimed to be a composer, but I never heard a single song. Walter was jive.

Mom and I were miscommunicating. I came at her the wrong way. I was argumentative and negative while she was miserable and distant. I didn't know how to properly express my concern for her. We tried as best we could, but our relationship wasn't working.

In spite of that, we shared some intimate moments. At my request, Mom was with me in Venice when I got my first tattoo. I had it put on my leg. She tried to warn me that I'd eventually tire of the thing, but what can you tell a headstrong fifteen-year-old? Inside the tattoo parlor I winced through the pain, all the while appreciating how Mom, despite her disapproval, hung in there with me.

If I was hurt by the Mike/Dee Dee episode, it couldn't compare to the hurt Mom was going through with Walter. It came to a head one morning when Walter took their arguments one step further.

I often listened at their door, worried that the punk might actually be hitting Mom. I asked her repeatedly, but she denied it. I didn't see any bruises, so I believed her. But this time I knew things had gotten out of hand. This time I heard him threatening her. I put my ear against the door. My heart started pounding when I heard scuffling just before Mom screamed, "Take your hands off me!" That was it. I let loose with a blood-curdling scream and busted down the door. There was Walter, holding my mom on the floor with his knee on her back. My scream was so loud, so fierce—*"GET OFF HER, YOU MOTHERFUCKER, OR I'LL CALL THE COPS!"*—that, like a scared rabbit, he jumped off her, ran upstairs, packed a bag, and split.

After he left, I worried he'd come back. I didn't want to take a chance, so I asked a few friends from Los Angeles, guys I trusted, to stay at the house with us. Walter never returned. In fact, he never showed his sorry ass again. I was convinced that was the end of Mom and her romantic relationships for a long time to come. I was wrong.

· · ·

My mother and I have this in common: quick courtships. We fall fast. I didn't see it then, but I do now. At the time, I gave my mother grief when, only a few months after Walter, she started dating a man she had met at church. His name is Carl Anderson and, unlike Walter, Carl is a legitimate citizen of the world. When Mom first encountered Carl, he already had an illustrious career. Carl can sing anything—jazz, r&b, pop, you name it. He owns the Judas role in *Jesus Christ Superstar*, both in the movie and the live musical that toured the world. Carl has recorded dozens of critically acclaimed records, had big hits, and earned an international reputation. He's a great artist, but when he started courting my mother, I had no interest in any of his accomplishments. All I saw was Mom moving too fast with no time out for reassessment. I was convinced the woman had no sense; I had had enough; I couldn't hold my tongue.

"Why hook up with another guy so soon?" I asked her. "Are you afraid of being alone?"

"Don't talk to me like that. That's my business, Laila, not yours."

"You still haven't learned you don't need a man to be happy."

"You're a child. You don't know what you're talking about."

"I know more than you think."

I was unrelenting in my criticism. Mom was right.

I was into her business, still reversing roles, acting like a parent and playing the protector.

I was scared she'd get hurt again and expressed my fear as rage, trying to control my mother, trying to control the world around me so it wouldn't fall apart again. But after what I'd seen her go through, I felt like I needed to put some sense in her head. The reality, though, was that she was the adult, not me. She was going to do what she was going to do.

My bad behavior didn't stop. I kept stealing her car. When she was asleep, I rolled it down the driveway and then took off for L.A. I was also antagonistic toward Carl. It wasn't long before he moved into our house—which only added to my resentment. No matter how charming or talented Carl might be, I didn't want to see his face every day. I felt it was too soon for him to be part of our household. He hadn't proved himself.

Understandably he didn't care for my attitude. He tried to communicate with me, but I was beyond reach. We were off to a lousy start.

I didn't see the wisdom I'd later learn to love in the house of worship both Mom and Carl attended, the Agape Science of the Mind Church. It took years for the creed to sink in. I'd attend sporadically but my head was elsewhere. Mom and Carl *did* meet in a spiritual place; they *did* have a spiritual connection. But I felt my mother was still vulnerable and could easily be taken advantage of again.

I wasn't happy to learn Carl and Mom were marrying. It was all happening too quickly. Like it or not, an elaborate wedding ceremony took place at our house in Malibu. Dr. Michael Beckwith, the founding minister at Agape, presided. More than a hundred friends attended. Mom looked radiant. I remained skeptical. I kept to myself. I remained angry when I learned that Carl and Mom were selling the Malibu house and buying one in Venice. Sure, I wanted to move—I'd always wanted to get the hell out of Malibu—but that didn't keep me from accusing Mom of subservience.

"The only reason you're moving to Venice is because Carl likes Venice," I said. "You're only doing it to please Carl. What about pleasing yourself?"

"You should be happy, Laila. You've always wanted to be closer to L.A."

Mom had a point. My life would be made easier by the move. Venice was fifteen minutes away from L.A, but I just wanted to see my mother in control. I wanted her calling the shots. Coincidentally, I was also seeing how Lonnie was definitely calling the shots when it came to my dad. That also disturbed me. When she and Dad came to town, Lonnie would call us and let us know where they were staying. Hana and I cherished the time we spent with our father. Despite his illness, he was still an overgrown kid. He still didn't know our ages, still wanted to smother us with kisses, still didn't know what was going on in our lives, still insisted on ordering ice cream from room service—in spite of his doctor's no-dairy warning. "You ain't the boss of me!" he'd declare, half serious, half joking. "I'll order what I want." And he did.

I saw my sophomore year as a new beginning. I was looking forward to going to a new school. I even got a new hairdo, a short cut that made me feel more mature. It was a clean look; I was looking for a clean start.

Hana and Alice had been going to Hamilton High where they seemed to be having fun. I knew there were cliques, but I figured I'd find my own place. Besides, I was happy to be leaving LACES and starting out fresh.

I was over at Alice's a month before school started when I felt the first twinge of trouble. Alice was on the phone with a girl reputed to be the roughest sista at Hamilton. For some reason, this girl had attitude about me and was talking mess. She was telling Alice how she had every intention of kicking my butt. "If she's talking about me," I said, "let her say it to me."

I got on the phone.

"I hear you think you're all that," said the girl I'll call Big Eva.

"I don't think anything."

"Well, don't think you can just stroll over to Hamilton and be cool. Because you can't. I don't want you there. If you show up that first day, I'll whup you."

"Tell you what," I said, "not only will I show up that first day, but I'll personally come over and introduce myself to you. That way you don't have to go looking for me."

"You don't know who you talking to."

"I ain't talking to anyone." And with that, I hung up the phone in her ear.

When the first day of school came around, I was ready. Because Hana had preceded me at Hamilton, no one quite knew what to make of me. Hana was sweet; I was fire. Hana was friendly; I was reserved. I gave off a don't-mess-with-me attitude. I wasn't interested in joining any clique.

I've always gone my own way.

Alice and Hana were my only friends—and that was enough. In fact, I was with Alice and Hana when I had that first encounter. We were heading toward the main entrance of Hamilton High.

A group of seven or eight tough-looking girls were hanging out on the steps. They all had atttiudes. The biggest among them had a deep cut across her face. I wouldn't call her pretty.

"That's Big Eva," whispered Alice. I figured as much.

I walked over to Big Eva and stood right there, toe to toe.

"I'm Laila."

Big Eva started rolling her neck, chewing gum and scowling like she wanted to fight. I still didn't know why. I didn't care. I wasn't budging.

"I told you I'd introduce myself," I said. "So here I am."

"Girl," she said, "you don't know who you're messing with."

Her girls closed ranks and started moving in on me. I still didn't budge. That's when the bell rang.

"After school," said Big Eva. "I'll be looking for you."

"I'll save you the trouble. I'll meet you right here."

Word got out. The whole school was buzzing with anticipation. Big Eva, who wouldn't back down, and Laila Ali, who wouldn't be intimidated, were going head to head.

When the final bell rang at three-thirty, I was back on the steps, waiting for Big Eva. A crowd had gathered. Everyone wanted action. My attitude was, *I was ready for whatever*. When Eva didn't show up, I was half relieved, half disappointed. I started walking to Taco Bell, and a large group walked with me. After a few steps, I looked across the street and saw Big Eva and her girls, heading for the same place. A large group also trailed them. It was a scene out of *Grease*.

When we got to Taco Bell, I ordered, then found a seat on one side of the restaurant. Eva's gang sat on the other. I wasn't

sure what she wanted to do, but I didn't care. I was going to
let her make the first move, since she had the problem with me.
I sat and ate my taco. Hana, Alice, and I sat there for a good
half hour. By then the place was packed with Hamilton students
waiting for a brawl. I felt a hundred eyes on me. When I was
through eating, I got up, slowly walked past Eva's table, and,
without saying a word, dumped my garbage in the trash bag.
Eva kept rolling her neck, but she never made a move. Nothing
happened . . . until the next day.

I was in the girls' room when Big Eva showed up.

"You're all show and no go," she said.

"Fine," I said. "Let's go."

She shoved me hard. I shoved her back harder. And just as
we were about to get cracking, a teacher walked through the
door. A few seconds later, we were sitting in the principal's
office.

The principal started a long speech about the futility of fighting. I interrupted her.

"Look," I said directly to Big Eva, "I'm not interested in fighting. I never was. I just wasn't about to be bullied. What makes
you think you can go around here bullying everyone?"

I expected Eva to start talking more mess. But instead, something amazing happened. Big Eva started crying. I mean, big
tears. Maybe it was because the door was closed and we were
alone in that office; maybe because she'd been holding it in so
long; or maybe because she sensed I wasn't really angry at her.
Whatever the reason, in between tears she let loose all the reasons she'd been acting the bully. All her tears and fears came

spilling out—about how she hated being overweight, how she felt ugly inside, how she never got any attention at home, how the only way she beat back bad feelings was by intimidating others, how deep down she really hated herself and the ugly front she created to scare off the world.

I was shocked by Big Eva's gut-honest revelations. And also moved—so moved that I shed a few tears myself. I knew she was being honest; I could feel all the hurt this girl had suffered. I even put my arms around her and let her cry in my arms. Soon we were both sobbing. It was crazy. Two girls who, twenty minutes earlier, were ready to fight were now acting like long-lost sisters. In its own way, it was beautiful. I'm not saying she reformed and joined the Girl Scouts, but the chip was off her shoulder. From that day on, Big Eva and I were cool.

The incident with Big Eva did not, however, turn me into a model student. I was still deep into my rebellion. I started smoking weed, which did nothing to increase my clarity. Weed can be fun, make you giggle, put the world in a weird light, even trigger creative thoughts. But weed also throws things out of focus. At fifteen going on sixteen, focus is just what I needed. Weed pushed me in the wrong direction. As a result, my grades and attendance suffered.

It was Christmastime, just before my sixteenth birthday. I was in a good mood. Mike was back on the scene. When he first started calling, I was reluctant. He had dogged me once, and once was enough. But I couldn't help but be happy that he finally kicked Dee Dee to the curb. And I also couldn't help but be drawn to the sweetness in Mike, his essential kindness that attracted me in the first place. Sure, he had tried to be a playa, but what young man doesn't go through that stage?

"Look," he said, with so much sincerity I felt myself melting, "I thought I wanted to be with her. But when we broke up, I realized I lost a friendship—our friendship—that meant a lot to me. I've been missing you all year. Dee Dee never understood me, not like you understand me. Besides, I never loved her. When I lost you, Laila, I lost more than a beautiful girl; I lost my soul mate. Give me another chance."

I was moved, but I told Mike it was too soon. He saw I needed time. Over time, I came to believe his apology was sincere. Little by little, we started seeing each other; little by little, he regained my trust. But I never forgot how he had hurt me in the past.

Mike was on my mind while I was walking through the Westside Pavilion, where he and I first met. I was with Alice and another girl I'll Tiffany. The mall was lavishly decorated for the holidays, and we were all feeling festive. We walked into a department store and started talking about buying Christmas gifts for our moms.

"*Buy?*" said Tiffany. "I ain't *buying* nothing. In this store you just *take* what you want."

I told her not to steal around me—to do it on her own time. If she was caught, I didn't want to be nailed as her accomplice.

At the same time, the thought of theft had been planted inside my head. I might not have been willing to get arrested on her account, but I toyed with the idea of stealing my own stuff. As we went off in different directions, I saw Alice and Tiffany slip a few silk nightgowns in their purses. A few minutes later, I acted on impulse; I put a tank top, one I was certain Mom would like, into my shopping bag. Nothing to it. It was an act of colossal stupidity, especially since I had money to pay for the thing. But good sense left me. The three of us were calmly walking out when fate, in the form of a blue-suited undercover officer, stepped in.

"Excuse me, young ladies," he said. "You'll have to come with me."

My first instinct was to turn back the hands of time, put the tank top back, and go home. But it was too late. The smirk on my face hid my embarrassment. Meanwhile, Alice and Tiffany were hysterical, sobbing as though we'd been caught in the act of murder. I stayed silent. I really wasn't scared. I figured—*I was stupid, I stole, I got caught*. No one does jail time for stealing a tank top.

At the police station, Alice and Tiffany begged to be let off; they swore never to do such an awful thing again. I just sat there. I knew attention would naturally focus on me because of my father. So I hid my identity by using Carl's last name.

"How about you?" the officer said, looking at me. "What do you have to say for yourself?"

I just shrugged my shoulders. I didn't want to give him the pleasure of watching me beg.

SEPARATING RIGHT FROM WRONG

When we got to court, I was intent on maintaining my composure. I couldn't help but worry, though, when the judge looked at me differently than he looked at my friends. His name was Roosevelt F. Dorn, a black man with a reputation for taking his job seriously. They said he ran his juvenile court with an iron hand. He said Alice and Tiffany were guilty of petty theft, but then dropped the charges. Then he turned his attention to me. He studied me sternly while I just stood there, slouched, still determined to show no fear. He studied my report for a long time. Too long.

"It is indicated," he said, "that you stole this merchandise by putting it in a large shopping bag. The arresting officer notes that you entered the store with a shopping bag, which is proof of your intention to steal. That's why the charge against you is graver than petty theft. You're charged with burglary."

I gulped.

"Because this is your first offense, I'm going to grant you a year's probation. In that time, however, you are not to associate with anyone on probation, stay out past nine, and you must maintain a passing average in school. Any violation of those mandates will result in severe repercussions. You'll be subject to periodic checks. In short, you have entered the juvenile court system. I trust that you will regard this regrettable turn of events with the utmost seriousness."

Unfortunately I didn't.

FINDING

PURPOSE

L ife went on.

Mom, Carl, Hana, and I moved into a house in Venice. It was a dramatic modern structure on one of the famous Venice canals. Everyone called it fabulous, a home out of an architecture book. When it came to decorating, Mom had flawless taste. The house was built on two large lots. A raised living room looked out onto the fairy-tale bridge and a canal filled with ducks. At any given day, you could see strolling tourists admiring the unique urban landscape.

For all the beauty of our surroundings, I still didn't accept Carl as part of the family. I was still angry at Mom for remarrying so soon. I was also angry at Hana for inviting kids over who, to my way of thinking, had no business in our house. Hana was naive; she trusted the world, considered everyone her friend, and, as a result, could be exploited. My attitude about friends was different—they were few and far between. I knew many so-called friends were drawn to us only because of our last name.

Several of these friends were at a party Hana gave when Mom and Carl were out of town. I suspected that some of the guys were stealing objects right out of our living room. When the party got out of hand, I ordered everyone out. When the guys refused, I went to Mom's room and returned with her loaded pistol. (Mom had taken shooting lessons.) I pointed straight at them; *"The party's over."* The guys left.

Meanwhile, my high school career continued downhill. My pattern of switching from school to school hadn't changed. I transferred from Hamilton to Culver City High where, if anything, I was more miserable. Culver City had new faces but the story was the same. I didn't seem to fit in anywhere.

I don't suppose high school is easy for anyone. It comes at a time when we're half kid and half adult. We don't know who we are. We're rattled by strong sexual feelings; our minds are too preoccupied to focus on schoolwork; we're tempted to conform to everything, even nonconformity.

A certain girl always talked trash behind my back, boasting how she was going to whup me. Well, one thing I couldn't stand was someone running their mouth and not backing it up. The day came around—in fact, the last day of school—when she swore she'd crush me. I saw her in the yard and figured it was time. "All right," I said. "Now's your chance." She was so scared she ran to the parking lot where she locked herself in a car. I kicked the car repeatedly, rocking it from side to side before finally giving up. She never did get out of the car. Later, though, she reported my rage to the principal, who promptly threw me out.

Mom and Carl had every right to be concerned.

I was running my own show and didn't care what they had to say about it.

They concluded that a boarding school might help. Next thing I knew Mom was driving me up Interstate 101 to Santa Barbara, all the while talking up this exclusive school where I might finally find some discipline. A part of me liked the idea of being away and starting out fresh.

When we arrived, the school officials were charming and accommodating. They took us on tour. But I immediately saw the whole setup as too white bread. It was like a summer camp for rich kids. I'd go crazy. I was honest with Mom.

"Make me stay here," I said, "and I'll just have one of my friends come get me."

When Mom learned the hefty tuition was nonrefundable, that was the end of boarding school in Santa Barbara.

Meanwhile, Mike honored his word and proved to be a true friend. We renewed our relationship and eventually our romance. This time he didn't play. We turned out to have a problem, but it had nothing to do with Mike's faithfulness. The problem went far deeper. When I was sixteen, I became pregnant.

Because we were comfortable in our relationship, we became careless. Mike's attitude was straight up: He encouraged me to have the baby. He said he'd support me. But he also left it up to me. It was a bad situation. Now I see it as another powerful reason for sexual restraint at an early age. Then I looked at it practically.

I simply couldn't see myself having a baby. I wasn't ready; I was too young. And besides, what would my family say? Just dealing with my regular emotions was all I could handle. I had no interest in being a "teen parent," which, in my young mind, I viewed negatively. I looked down on teen parenthood as a weak and helpless condition. I was intent on being strong and independent.

Looking back, I see that I handled the situation wrong. I had an abortion. I regret that decision. At the time, though, I lacked perspective. I wouldn't admit what I was doing to myself and to my child. It wasn't that I was pro abortion. I hated the idea. But I did believe in a woman's right—my right—to make the decision.

My decision was excruciatingly painful. My mind was racing

a million miles an hour: *Don't think about what you're doing. It's just an operation. Millions of abortions are performed every year. Do it fast before this thing inside you turns into a baby; get it over with. It's okay. It's perfectly reasonable. It's fine.*

It was hell. Mike drove me to the doctor's office where he paid for the procedure and waited. On the operating table, drifting in and out of consciousness, I couldn't help but think about what was happening. I wondered what I'd be feeling three years from now when my child would have been three years old. I couldn't deny the emotional reality—something inside me was dying. Thoughts of death darkened my mind as I bled, doubled over with cramps, throwing up, crying in pain.

Mike was really strained by the situation, but remained steady. He drove me home and made sure I was okay. I wouldn't tell Mom about this for another year. I wouldn't tell anyone. I simply went to my bedroom and stayed under the covers all afternoon, all night, all the next day. I said I had a cold; I called it the flu. Mike was sweet. He called and came by to visit. But I didn't feel like talking. It was a lonely, disheartening ordeal. It saddened me to the core of my soul. Recovery came slowly. It ruined the romance between me and Mike—at least for a long while.

Yet I can't say I fell apart. Or even came close to falling apart. I knew I needed something to keep me rooted in reality. The painful experience made me more responsible. I realized it was time to get it together and take control of my future. I swore I'd never work for anyone for $5 an hour. I wanted a pleasant lifestyle and knew being in business for myself was the means to that end. I'd always been fascinated with sculptured nails, even setting up shop at home when I was in the seventh grade. Now I was sixteen and old enough to get a license.

I went to the Yellow Pages where I found schools for hair and nails. I chose nails because there was already an over-abundance of hair stylists and, besides, accreditation for hair required sixteen hundred hours in contrast to the four hundred needed for nails. Despite my problems at school and the pain of the abortion, I never lost sight of my mandate to my mother, first announced when I was twelve: By the time I was eighteen, I was moving out and going to college. If I were to meet that goal—and nothing could stop me—I needed a way to make money. Becoming a manicurist was the answer.

Pursuing the goal took motivation. And, trust me, I had motivation to burn. I started out in a school in the heart of black L.A. on Crenshaw Boulevard. I went five days a week, taking a one-hour bus ride every day after school. I rode from Culver to Crenshaw where I studied manicuring from four in the afternoon till nine at night. I was loving it and, in fact, had accumulated half the hours required—over two hundred—when I went to visit my dad in Michigan.

The older I got, the more challenging those visits became. My father had strong beliefs about how I should carry myself. He'd make comments like, "You shouldn't be wearing those kinds of tank tops" or "Your jeans are too tight. No Muslim daughter of mine should be running around in clothes that tight."

I'd have to remind him that, for all the respect I gave his

religion, it wasn't my religion. Besides, he wasn't involved enough in my life to be telling me what I should and should not be wearing. The discussions would break off before they got ugly. I'd firmly stand my ground until Dad would shake his head and say, "You can't tell Laila anything. She's just like me."

When I came back from Michigan I discovered the nail school had lost my hours. Don't ask me how, but their records were destroyed, and they insisted I start over. I thought I'd die. I'd spent months riding the bus and staying extra hours to build up those credits. I'd be damned if I was going to lose that time. But there was nothing to do. Their inefficiency infuriated me, but it didn't stop me. I was determine to finish what I started. I hauled out the Yellow Pages again and found a beauty school in Culver City where I enrolled and started from scratch. One way or the other, I was going to develop a marketable skill.

I could have said the hell with it and quit. But I learned a valuable lesson:

Success is built on a foundation of hard work.

Success is about staying focused. Never quitting. Overcoming obstacles. Obstacles will inevitably appear, but if you're sure of

what you're doing and steady in your pursuit, you will overcome them. The strength of your conviction will knock them
down.

I had more in mind than simply working in a salon. I had a
vision of a chain of salons. I saw myself as an entrepreneur,
setting up a number of high-end manicure centers from one end
of the state to the other—and beyond. Mom encouraged me.
She was the first and best set of hands on which I experimented.
She never doubted the sincerity of my efforts, and though her
interests were far more intellectual, she never looked down on
mine. She understood me—and loved me—well enough to support my plan. She respected my practicality.

I was impatient to get going. Fortunately I found the patience
to plow my way through the manicuring course for the second
time. I was less patient, however, when it came to driving. Like
most teens, I couldn't wait; I was obsessed with getting a car. I
was tired of sitting at the bus stop waiting around forever. Driving represented independence, which is why I spent endless
hours pestering my mother for a car. She had the good sense to
refuse, but I lacked the good sense to leave it there. If Mom
wouldn't get me a car, I'd get one on my own.

I decided to act when my girls and I learned about a party
we had no way to get to. "Don't worry," I said, "I'm buying a
car." I found a 1977 Toyota Celica in a *Recycler* ad. I scraped
together the money, got on the bus with my friends, rode over
to Century City, and met the man with the Toyota. The thing
was rusty and raggedy. I didn't care. It was a car. I drove it once
around the block to make sure it ran. It did. So I paid the man

his $400, and we all piled in. "You ladies ready?" I asked. "Let's go!" they replied. All smiles, I turned the key in the ignition—and waited. And waited. And waited some more. Nothing. The thing was dead. I looked down the street for the man who'd pocketed my money, but he was long gone. I wanted to kill him; I felt like a fool.

A few minutes later, some guys came by and saw our distress. They looked under the hood, jiggled some wires, and got it started. Finally we were off. We'd get to this party come hell or high water. But my junk-mobile had other ideas. It started steaming and smoking until I couldn't see out the windshield. I pulled in a gas station where a mechanic pointed to a hole in the cooling pipe. It needed water. Fact is, it needed water every twenty minutes. At that rate, it took us an hour to drive five miles. When we arrived at the party we looked like war refugees. I kept that nasty Toyota two weeks—never buying insurance or even registering the thing. Finally, it broke down for good, and I ditched it on the street. I was content to let the monster rot.

The summer before our junior year, Alice, Tiffany, and I decided to go to Crenshaw High. I had never gone to an all-black school before, and the idea intrigued me. Crenshaw had a reputation for being the happening school. Besides, that's where the fine brothers went. People warned me it was rough, but I paid no attention. I had a notion of myself as superwoman. I was invincible. Besides, it was just summer school.

Enrollment day rolled around. We were waiting in line to register when a girl approached us whom I knew had transferred from Hamilton. She'd been sweet on a guy who'd been sweet on me. She didn't like me and didn't mind letting me know. She accused us of cutting in line. The accusation was false, and I let her know it.

"If you have a problem with me," she said, "we can handle it."

"You're the one with a problem."

"Well, what's up then?"

Next thing I knew, four other girls from the neighborhood crowded around her. I saw we were in the wrong territory to be disputing anything, but pride kept me from backing down.

"All right," I said. "You can all line up and wait your turn. I'm not fighting y'all at once."

My call for a fair fight seemed reasonable. I was confident, in spite of the fact that my support slipped away as Tiffany and Alice disappeared in the background.

We took it outside. I expected the girls to move on me immediately, but for some reason they stalled. I didn't understand why until I heard the screech of tires and saw a car come to an abrupt stop in front of the school. A big muscular man jumped out. He ran up the steps to where we were standing. As he ran, I saw a gun tucked in his pants.

"Someone called and said you been messing with my sister," he told me.

"You got it wrong. Your sister has been messing with me."

Before I could blink, he hauled off and punched me in the

mouth. I rocked back, but I didn't go down. I wouldn't give him the satisfaction. But I also wasn't stupid; I wasn't about to retaliate.

Watching what he did, Alice cried, "Man, that's messed up."

Then he kicked Alice in the stomach.

"So this is how you do it around here," I said.

Just for good measure, he kicked me in the gut. I still stood my ground. My lip was swollen; blood was pouring out of my mouth. My head was hurting, my stomach badly bruised, but my thoughts were clear. I wasn't scared. I wasn't about to beg for mercy. I was determined to stand there, look the asshole in the eye, and show no fear. At the same time, I knew we were outnumbered and I wasn't ready to die over this BS.

After a silent standoff, he walked back to his car and roared off. We decided not to enroll at Crenshaw High after all. Six months later, when I saw the girl who started the ugly mess walking through the Beverly Center mall, I decided not to jump on her right there and then. I wasn't interested in perpetuating a vicious cycle.

By summer's end, I decided to try still another school, Venice High, because it was close to home.

I made one friend who was gay, a guy I'll call Andre. Andre was nice. We'd hang out during PE and walk the track together. I didn't get into his business and he didn't get into mine. Our conversations were easy. He was quick and witty and made me laugh. I didn't feel like he was judging me, and I sure wasn't judging him.

One afternoon during our walk around the track we heard a

voice crying out, "Look at the faggot! Look at how the sissy walks like a girl!"

As we got closer to the bleachers, we saw the words were coming from a girl who had once been a friend. We weren't hanging out anymore, and now I knew why. She was ignorant.

"Forget her," I told Andre. We walked on, but the insults got louder. And uglier. It wasn't just "faggot" and "sissy," but nasty descriptions of how she imagined Andre had sex.

Andre was small. Probably didn't weigh 120. His tormentor was more my size—5 feet 11 and 170 pounds plus. She was screaming loud enough for half the school to hear. I decided to shut her up. I left the track and walked to where she was sitting.

"If you got a problem with my friend," I said, "then you got a problem with me."

"You gonna whup me?"

"I'm gonna do whatever I need to do to shut your ignorant mouth."

A minute later, it was on and cracking.

She went for my hair and managed to pull out some strands from my braids. But I managed to put her in a headlock. I also managed to pull her arm out of its socket. She was screaming, "I got her hair! I got her hair!" As she was screaming, though, they were sliding her in an ambulance and rushing off to some hospital. I got suspended.

As a high schooler, you couldn't categorize me. You couldn't call me a bad girl because I avoided gangs and heavy drugs. I also didn't sleep around. But I was hardly a Girl Scout. It wasn't my schoolmates, though, who saw the worst of my behavior. It was Mom who bore the brunt of my rebelliousness. I came and went as I pleased, and when she tried to discipline me I laughed in her face.

I did what many of us do; I took out my frustrations on the one I loved most.

Feeling my unhappiness, Mom often blamed herself, saying, "I've been a terrible mother." That very statement would turn me around. I'd drop my anger and become a reassuring parent. "No," I'd insist, "you've been a good mother. I understand how much you've been through. I love you."

I did. And I do. Yet all the love in the world didn't keep me from making still another major mistake. But maybe "mistake" is the wrong word. Maybe there are no mistakes—only lessons. If that's the case, this lesson stung like no other. This lesson was about being locked up.

Round
8

LEARNING
THE HARD
WAY

Fate is funny—the people you meet, the time you meet them, and the consequences you face. Fate is also fickle. Some of those meetings come at the perfect time; other hookups are disastrous. Mostly, though, I believe fate is what you make it.

I was sixteen, going on seventeen, and my year's probation was just about up. Carl and I were finally getting along. My life was improving. In fact, this was the final day of my probation. Day 365. All I had to do was get through another twenty-four hours and I'd be free with a slate clean. Only a couple of weeks earlier I'd completed my four hundredth hour—six hundred if you count the lost records from my original school—and passed my state board for manicure accreditation. The all-day test was grueling. I used my mother as my model and, despite my nervousness, passed with flying colors. It was helpful to have my mom as part of the test. She supported me all the way. Now I was licensed and able to do what I had long dreamed—earn money.

You'd think I'd chill out on this final day. You'd think I'd chill at the beach or go to a movie or just hang with old friends. But none of that happened. I was anything but cool. I blew it. Big time.

It happened on a Friday. I'd ditched school and was with a guy I'd been dating for a few weeks. He was older, twenty-two or twenty-three, and still lived with his parents. Nice guy, but someone I didn't know very well. He said he'd take me shopping. "I'll buy you whatever you want," he offered. "Whatever you need."

I didn't need a thing. I had clothes galore, but at that age my mind-set was *the more the better*. I couldn't have enough cute outfits. I was plain greedy.

We went to the Gap in Beverly Hills. "It's my treat," he said.

I picked out whatever I wanted, maybe a thousand dollars' worth of stuff. If I had been thinking straight, I would have questioned him. He wasn't independently wealthy; he didn't even have his own place. Where was this money coming from? At that moment, I didn't care. The clothes were piled high on the checkout counter.

"Use this," he said, handing me a credit card.

"Whose is it?" I asked.

"My mom's."

"Your mom's?" I questioned.

"She lets me use it."

I could have questioned the appropriateness of using his

mother's card to buy me clothes, but I didn't. I was so eager to get the clothes, my common sense went blank. I handed the clerk the card.

He and I hadn't driven more than a few blocks when we were stopped by the police. The cops quickly separated us, but before they did, the guy whispered to me, "Don't tell them anything." That's when I knew something was wrong.

We were arrested and questioned at the Beverly Hills police station where we were told the charge was credit card fraud.

Whether I liked it or not, I was implicated. I was the one who gave the clerk the card. It turned out that the guy had previous convictions. The police quickly learned I was still on probation, and a trial date was set for three weeks.

I was in deep trouble, but deeper denial.

I didn't think the judge would do anything after I explained my innocence. My court-appointed attorney seemed little more concerned than me. My mother was understandably distressed. She couldn't understand what I was doing in this situation. I couldn't either. It was a lapse of judgment. For the three weeks before the trial, I went to school, looked for work at a salon, and led my normal life. No more hanging out with people I didn't know.

Mom and Carl came to the trial in Inglewood. I was careful to dress conservatively. The guy was already in jail, but that still didn't worry me because he had a criminal history. I had only one minor shoplifting episode. I walked into juvenile court with my head high. I was prepared to pay a fine. I was prepared for an extended probation. Mainly I was prepared for a party some friends were throwing that night. I was still superwoman, and superwoman wasn't about to be fazed by an appearance in court.

I stood before the same judge as before, the formidable Roosevelt F. Dorn. He questioned me briefly, sternly. I explained everything that had happened.

Judge Dorn looked at my probation papers and then looked at me. I didn't like the expression on his face. "Young lady," he said, "this is a far more serious offense than shoplifting. This is an attempt at a sophisticated crime." Then a long, long pause. It might have been a minute but seemed like an hour. Then Dorn dropped the bomb.

"I'm especially concerned," he said, "that you were still on probation while engaging in this fraud. Something isn't right here. I sense little if any rehabilitation on your part. I'm not certain of what to do. I want time to consider your final sentence. In the interim, I'm ordering you to juvenile hall. I'll see you in a month."

The gavel came crashing down. I came crashing down. I stood there, stupefied, stunned, speechless. My heart started slamming against my chest; I turned to see my mother, who was crying. I turned to my lawyer.

"He can't do this, can he?" I asked.

"He can do anything he pleases."

Juvenile hall. The reality set in. *I'm getting locked up.*

"When?" I asked my lawyer. "When do I have to go?"

A police officer answered my question. He put my hands behind my back, snapped on a pair of cuffs, and walked me out of the courtroom.

It was the scariest, most humiliating moment of my life.

I was helpless. I had no control over anything. I looked back at my mother, but there was no time to say good-bye.

Along with a dozen other prisoners, I was put on a bus, chained up, and driven to the women's bungalow in juvenile hall. The other girls were gabbing, but I was still in shock. The bus had bars on the windows. I couldn't see outside, couldn't believe this was happening. *What about the party I was supposed to attend tonight? What about my life? This isn't how the story goes. This is impossible. I'm not the kind of girl who goes to jail. I told the judge what happened; the judge was supposed to believe me. I'm not supposed to be here.*

But who was I talking to? Only myself. No one was listening. No one was helping. The bus was pulling up to juvenile hall. And I was being escorted inside.

From the start, Mom had advised me to use Carl's name—Anderson—and not Ali. She didn't want the press coming down and reporting on Ali's daughter. Her plan worked. The press never showed, but it didn't take long for the girls to learn who I was. A girl from school, already incarcerated in the same locale, spread the word. When I arrived, I was wearing some gold jewelry, a few bracelets and rings. I had to turn them over and then strip. All this happened in an open area with everyone looking. I was humiliated. My own mother had not seen me naked in years, much less strangers. I had to pull down my panties and cough to make sure I wasn't hiding anything inside me. I was given county-issued underwear, yellow jail pants, a white work shirt. I used a public shower with all the other girls. The toilet stalls had no doors. When I went to the bathroom, I was on full display. There was one enormous room accommodating all the bunks. Fifty girls slept in that room. And you can imagine the different attitudes. I kept my don't-mess-with-me facade in full force. I was not overly friendly. On that level, I had no problems.

Emotionally, though, I had nothing but problems. I spent the first week crying. I worried that my mother didn't know where I was; I worried I'd get lost in the criminal justice system. If my world could flip upside down, as it had in court, it could flip again. Anything could happen. I wasn't safe. I was vulnerable. Superwoman was scared.

LEARNING THE HARD WAY

The staff was rough. If you talked out of turn you got a quick, "Shut your mouth!" If you had a complaint about the rotten food, "Stuff it!" If you wanted to talk a second more during your three-minute phone call, "Forget it!" There was no rule bending, no sympathetic counselors, no words of reassurance. I tried to avoid going to the bathroom as much as possible, but what can you do? How long can you hold it in? My little middle-class niceties were gone.

The staff said I looked like the saddest girl in the world. It took many days to finally make friends with another prisoner, a Latina who had a story similar to mine. But as soon as I found a friend I could relate to, the system dropped another bomb: I was being transferred to a juvenile hall in Sylmar. They didn't say why. One morning they simply said, "Get on the bus."

It was another bus with bars, another instance when I was chained to the other girls. I worried whether they'd told my mother that I was changing jails. I asked. "Who knows? Who cares?" was the reply. Sylmar was rougher than Central. The girls were raunchier and the staff meaner. I got lucky; I was locked up in a cell that, oddly enough, I liked. At least I had my own sink and toilet. I didn't have to deal with the other girls. Mom visited on Sundays and brought books on meditation and prayer. Mom, Carl, and Hana hung in there with me. During this whole time, Dad and I had no contact. I read *Wanderlust* by Danielle Steele, a love story that helped me escape my surroundings. My mind was focused on getting out. I'd cross off each day. Days seemed long as months, weeks long as years.

The third week finally came around. The time had finally

passed, the day finally arrived. I didn't need any more jail time. I had learned my lesson the moment Judge Dorn said the words "juvenile hall." I had my speech all prepared. *I understand, Your Honor; I'm a new person; I served my time and learned my lesson; just let me out.* All I could think about was how the nightmare was over. I imagined myself back home with my mother, calling my friends, eating edible food, having my life back. That morning I scrubbed my face, brushed my teeth, took one last look at the place, walked to the bus, didn't mind when they chained us together, didn't mind the long drive from Sylmar to Inglewood. At least I knew where I was going: home.

They say expectations will kill you. They say hope for everything and expect nothing. Such thoughts were not in my head. I expected to get the hell out. What I didn't expect—and what crushed my spirit—was that Judge Dorn didn't even hear my case. He ran out of time. I just sat there in the back room, waiting and waiting and waiting. At five o'clock we were ushered back on the bus. That was it. I complained bitterly, but who was listening? "Happens all the time," someone said. "What does that mean? When will he consider my case?" A court clerk looked at a list and said, "A month from today."

I was incredulous. How could they tool me around like this? How could he make me stay inside for another whole month? My lawyer told me the judge could do what he wanted, but this was too much. Back to Sylmar for a couple of weeks, then back to Central. I can't say that I adjusted, but neither can I say I went crazy. I did what I had to do. I was evaluated by a shrink who said I had no mental problems. She thought I was coping rather well, but she couldn't see inside my head. My head was reverberating with one thought and one thought only—*please get me out of here!*

That second month passed slowly, but I made it through without incident. I managed to get on a privileged list of prisoners who were served fruit juice instead of milk. The arrival of my fruit juice every afternoon became the highlight of my day. The arrival of the day of reckoning found me positively joyful. Still another ride to Inglewood, another wait in the back room before being called by the judge. After an hour or so, my lawyer appeared.

"We have a problem," he said.

"Oh God." My heart sank.

"The judge isn't here today. Another judge has taken his place. We have a choice. We can take our chances with this new judge, or we can wait for Judge Dorn to return."

"How long will that take?"

"Three, four weeks."

"What will this new judge say?"

"That's just the point. He doesn't know you."

My instincts said wait for Judge Dorn. I felt that once he returned, he'd let me go home. I still thought I had it all figured out. So I waited. My hopes were long dashed for an early release, so why not wait a little longer? I didn't want to take a chance on a two-year jail sentence.

I realized impatience was my worst enemy. I needed to be cool.

I needed to chill for another month or so and bank on my lawyer's advice. So I went back and shuffled between Sylmar and Central and a third location, Sybil Brand, where I heard stories about roaches creeping in your ear and laying eggs while you slept. I hardly slept at all. The place was run down and overcrowded. At times girls were forced to sleep on the cafeteria floor. By now my attitude was *whatever*. I learned to cope. I also learned that time passes, whether you worry about it or not. You can't hurry it up or slow it down. You best find a groove that works for you. I can't say I adjusted with complete peace of mind, but I never went off. My tears turned to sighs. I waited that final month with less anxiety than the first two. I was more accepting of my fate and less anxious about controlling it. What will be will be.

The day finally arrived when I stood before Judge Dorn, the man known for issuing stinging bench warrants at the drop of a hat. He ran his courtroom with an iron hand. No matter what, my attorney assured me, the judge had my best interests at heart.

When I looked around the courtroom at the clerks and bailiffs, I saw in their eyes sympathy for me. Most of them knew I was the champ's daughter and felt sorry for my situation. They felt what I was going through.

Dorn's speech was brief. "Young lady," he said, "you haven't had enough guidance at home. To make sure you receive strict guidance, I'm putting you in placement."

I wasn't happy to hear this. My attorney had argued for a day program, meaning I could go home every night. Placement meant a live-in facility, exactly what I wanted to avoid. But Judge Dorn was not persuaded by my lawyer's claim that I was responsible. "Laila needs structure," he insisted. "Enforced structure." Now, though, I worried that placement could take months. I couldn't stand the idea of being in the system any longer. At the same time, Dorn was clearing my record. Time in placement would mean no criminal record of any kind. I was grateful for that—and still am.

"I'll have you placed in three days," the judge assured me. "You'll be in the facility for an extended period of time. Your release will be at their discretion. I suggest you give your heart and soul over to the placement program. Whatever you do, I never want to see you here again."

ACCEPTING
HELP

I was thin and pale. My energy was drained. At seventeen, after being locked up for three months, I still hadn't fully learned the lesson Judge Dorn had in mind. I didn't like placement. I didn't like the idea of being cut off from my family for at least another six months. When I entered the big Victorian mansion that served as the group home for Girls Republic, the placement center in Monrovia, a town east of Pasadena, I was convinced I didn't belong there. My initial attitude was *I'm getting out of here as quickly as humanly possible.* That attitude got me nowhere.

At least the transfer was immediate. The day after Judge Dorn's decision, Susan Kornbacher from Girls Republic interviewed me. She immediately concluded I was right for her program. Within an hour I had packed up my things in grocery bags, been released, and was seated next to Susan as she drove us to Monrovia. I sat and listened to Susan explain the program. In my mind, though, I viewed placement as something to put up with, not a place to grow. I also have to confess feeling superior to the other seven girls who lived in the house. Their situations seemed more serious than mine. I had merely been in the wrong place at the wrong time. I was above it all.

Out of eight girls, one other was black, one Mexican, one Asian, and the rest were white. The Mexican girl became my friend. She was younger, wilder, and in need of a big sister. She was one of the reasons my attitude began to change. The change, though, was slow in coming. I still harbored deep resentments. I'd attend the group therapy sessions, for example, and barely say a word. I remained skeptical and distant from my peers. The staff saw how I was holding back. I just wouldn't open up. They called it coasting. They put it to me plainly: The longer I refused to cooperate, the longer I'd be there. Understanding that, I finally got with the program.

I didn't mind the chores—making beds, mopping floors, cooking meals, cleaning windows. I actually enjoyed the domestic tasks. There was also a practical side to placement I appreciated. We learned basic bookkeeping principles that I found helpful and still utilize. It was the emotional stuff, though, that put me off—at least at first. I could help the other girls with their problems but couldn't accept help in return.

Funny, but if you hang around people long enough and hear them open their hearts, you start to change. Slowly but surely, your own heart starts to open. During the therapy session, I isolated myself in the back of the room; I folded my arms and crossed my legs; I closed my mind and stared into space, but certain stories got to me.

"I want to talk about my mother," said one of the girls. "I have a problem with my mother."

Don't we all? the wise guy inside me silently chided.

"When I tell my mother things," the girl explained, "she doesn't believe me."

"What sort of things?" asked the therapist.

There was a silence. Tears welled up in the girl's eyes. Her voice broke several times as she told the story. "My stepbrother comes over to the house all the time. Sometimes he sleeps over. One time he slept over when Mom was out of town. In the middle of the night he came in my bedroom . . ."

She started crying uncontrollably. Other girls in the group started crying. I couldn't help it; I was crying along with everyone else. I could relate.

Month after month she was raped. She kept telling her mother, but her mother didn't believe her. So the girl ran away from home and lived on the wild side. If you couldn't feel her story, you couldn't feel anything.

This gave another girl the courage to speak up.

"My father would wake me up when I was fast asleep. He made me go downstairs and stand in front of his friends. He put on rock music and made me take off my clothes. He charged people to watch me dance."

I didn't want to listen, but I had to. I didn't want to hear painful stories that scorched these girls' souls. In the intimacy

of the therapy room, in the heartbreaking honesty of these stories, my haughty attitude crumbled. Along with everyone else,
I broke down. I felt a pain that linked me to them. I felt part of
something, a spiritual connection. I started to recover.

I realized that people had gone through so much deeper pain and more horrible humiliation than I had.

My ordeal paled compared to theirs. I was never more aware of
the value of my own family, my own caring mother, and how
I had taken so much for granted.

I learned by listening. Not just listening with my ears but
with my heart. The kind of listening where someone knows you
care. You don't really have to say anything. You don't have to
say, "I understand," or "I've gone through the same thing," or

"things will get better." You just have to listen. You just have to be there.

A change came over me. My attitude changed from *how can I get out of there?* to *how can I help others?* My Mexican friend, for example, had been in a gang and refused to take off her bandanna, which, of course, was against house rules. She also snuck out to smoke weed. The regulations of Girls Republic required us to report any illegal activities. I was against tattling, so I didn't. But I did put private pressure on her to straighten up. "Why are you making problems for yourself?" I asked her. "If it makes you feel better, put on that bandanna when you go to bed. Just take it off when you wake up. Don't send up red flags. Be cool. If they catch you high, your ass is back in jail. All your progress will go down the drain."

After several months at placement, I became a foreman, which meant wider responsibilities. Several of the girls came to me for advice. I became close to the black sista who came from the projects. She had no support from her family—none—and spent all her time messing up. She refused to obey any rules. "Girl," I'd tell her, "why don't you just deal with the system? It takes less energy and, besides, you'll get out of here." But I soon saw that she kept rebelling because she *wanted* to go to the juvenile hall; juvenile hall was better than home; anything was better than home. After juvenile hall, she knew she'd be sent back here, a mansion where she'd eat decent food and wear decent clothes. Other girls who graduated faced the dim prospect of returning to homes where they were neither safe nor wanted. I wondered how they ever found the strength to leave the comfort of Girls Republic.

The program gave me something I always lacked—humility. I had to admit I needed help, that others had wisdom I lacked. I had to do things I didn't want to do. At first, walking with the girls and counselors at the local mall embarrassed the hell out of me. Later I saw it as humility. I was no better than anyone else. I was sent to placement, and our placement group was out for a stroll. If you want to stare, stare all you like. I had the same issue at the day school down the street. They looked down on us placement students. They knew who we were and taunted us with, "We get to go home after school. You don't."

I wanted to fight the brats, but it wasn't worth delaying going home. I later transferred to Canyon Continuation High School in Pacific Palisades, where, for the first time in my life, I was a straight-A student. I liked continuation because you worked at your own pace. I caught up with the schooling I'd missed. I was treated like an adult. Amazingly enough, I was taking my adult responsibilities seriously—my *emotional* responsibilities. I realized I'd been responsible for disrespecting my mother by taking my frustrations out on her. When I saw the problems of the other girls, mine seemed minor. Mom had been there for me during this whole ordeal. When after many months I finally earned weekend passes to go home, one of the requirements was to discuss certain issues with your family and report back to the group. Well, by then Mom and I were cool. I appreciated her more than I ever had. I tried to make amends, not just by saying I'm sorry but by amending my behavior. I began acting respectfully. In my mind, there weren't that many issues to discuss. I'd messed up. Now I was cleaning up—and that was it. Many times, to satisfy the program, I'd invent some issue that I supposedly thrashed out with my mother. In reality, though, Mom and I were mellow.

If I had one objection about placement—other than the tattling requirement—it concerned overanalysis. That methodology may apply more to whites than blacks. Black families, at least in my experience, don't scrutinize issues over and over. You say it once, you put it out there, and that's it. At placement, there was a tremendous amount of telling and retelling and retelling again. Everything was looked at from twelve different angles; every last detail of your day was put under a magnifying glass. After a while, the law of diminishing returns set in. Sometimes I thought the counselors were looking for meaning when there wasn't any.

At the same time, thank God for placement. Thank God for Judge Roosevelt F. Dorn, who was later elected mayor of Inglewood, largely because of his great work in successfully rehabilitating juveniles who came through his courtroom. The judge knew just what I needed. All that time I waited around in jail I didn't realize he really *did* have a plan for me. He really *did* have my best interests at heart.

By locking me up, he set me free.

By forcing me into placement, he placed me in a position where I could finally grow beyond anger and resentment. Before Girls Republic, I was ready to battle the world. Look at me wrong and I was ready to tear your head off. Now I learned to choose my battles carefully. Not everything was worth a physical or even verbal fight. Rather than confrontation, I learned appreciation. I learned to express gratitude. I saw strength isn't a matter of force, but confidence. I was starting to understand that true strength is rooted in the good feelings I have about myself. More and more, I was in touch with those feelings.

I think those feelings led me to call Mike. We had been writing and then, when phone privileges opened, I called him. Mike never judged me for what happened at the Gap. When we first discussed it, I said, "Look, I don't know what I was thinking. But that's behind me now." He saw I learned my lesson. I also saw that had I been with Mike the fiasco never would have happened. Mike didn't play cops-and-robbers. He had a good gig at a store where he'd been working for years. Mike took care of himself, stayed clean, and, most importantly, supported me while I was away. He had proven what I had long known to be true: As far as friends go, Mike was a prince.

When I earned weekend passes, I often went to Mike. He still shared an apartment with his mom, and I still felt comfortable hanging out. The business with Dee Dee was ancient history. After six months at the group home, I wanted to reconnect with the real world. Mike and his mom were real people offering me real support.

The raging storm inside me had subsided, perhaps even passed. That was the blessing of the group home. It was a place where I could ride out that storm, see it for what it was, and go on with my life. My soul was calmer, my spirit more at peace. I leaned heavily on my mother's spiritual teaching. I saw the world composed of positives and negatives. It was my choice to avoid negative energy fields.

It was evident that God wasn't out there, but rather in here.

Inside me. It was God—and the power of positive light—that led me to Judge Dorn and Monrovia. That was the light I needed to follow. Sometimes that light is strong, sometimes it's dim. It can shine or it can flicker. Sometimes it can disappear. There were moments in the following years when, in spite of this new consciousness, I lost the light altogether. There were times when I found myself stumbling in the dark.

For all I had learned in Monrovia, certain characteristics about me were unchanged. More than ever, I was set to strike out on my own. I was determined to make a mark. The independence I had dreamt of since I was a little girl was now within reach. I had every intention of grabbing it. Nothing could—or would—get in my way.

When I say something, I mean it.

"The minute I turn eighteen," I told Mom time and again, "I'm gone."

By December 30, 1995, my eighteenth birthday, I had moved out. I was finally on my own.

DEVELOPING

INDEPENDENCE

The idea of independence has haunted me as long as I can remember. Nothing seemed more important than doing my own thing on my own terms. I didn't see independence as an abstract concept or distant dream. I saw it as a practical plan that centered on the beauty business, a business I liked and understood.

I took the time to learn to do nails well. Extremely well. I knew it was something I could master. I wasn't fantasizing about being famous; I was just planning on being a successful businesswoman, nothing more or less.

The group home in Monrovia enforced the idea of self-reliance. I was helped along with some inheritance Mom had put aside for me when I reached eighteen. Once I graduated high school, I took that money and moved out of the house. Mike and I rented an apartment in Westchester. I selected the furniture and we split the rent.

DEVELOPING INDEPENDENCE

I found a salon in Beverly Hills that needed a manicurist. After working there, though, I realized their prices were too low and lacked the high-end clientele I expected. The owner was a diva who ran her shop like an uptight dictator; her rules had rules. I tried as best I could. I made flyers advertising my specialty—pink and white acrylics—and passed them all around the neighborhood. I was learning to promote myself while I continued honing my craft. My acrylics looked sensational but after a week or so might pop off. Not all my customers were satisfied. It took a while. But when I got it together, my customers were so pleased they'd bring in three of their friends.

Meanwhile, Miss Diva and I butted heads. She was always in my face. She had this rule, for example, about employees wearing black on Friday. One Friday I slipped up and wore dark gray. Miss Diva wasn't having it. I was working on a pedicure when I saw Miss Diva coming toward me. Her eyes were on fire.

"What is the meaning of this, Laila? Your attire is unacceptable."

"Excuse me," I said politely, "but I'm with a client."

"There's no excuse for insubordination."

"Can we please discuss this later—privately?"

"When you first came here I told you I have standards. A dress code is part of those standards. You've violated that code . . ."

My client looked at Miss Diva like she was crazy. I kept trying to avert the confrontation, but Miss Diva was insistent. "You're going to have go home and change."

"Into what?" the customer wanted to know.

"Friday is all-black day," I explained. "Dark gray is considered wild and crazy."

"I don't need your sarcasm," said Miss Diva.

"And you know what," I said, "I don't need your job."

With that, I was gone.

I wasn't going to be talked down to. And I wasn't going to be without a job for long. Within a week I found work at a salon in Marina del Rey, close to where I was living with Mike. The owner was a man who liked my energy and set me to work where I'd eventually replace a manicurist who was pregnant. The salon was a cute converted house. The upstairs, where the hair stylists worked, was tastefully decorated. Nails were downstairs, a separate space with a separate entrance.

When I arrived, there was a rickety table, a couple of old chairs, a dirty white tile floor, and no disinfectant. Within a few months I changed all that. I did some decorating—bought a little white couch from Pier One, a beautiful manicure table, put up my polish racks with a hundred different colors, hung soft blue mini blinds, and built up my clientele. Soon I got my business license and ordered an outside sign that said LAILA'S NAIL STUDIO. I made an agreement with the owner to sublease the space and run my own shop based on my own clientele. I paid him weekly rent and whatever I earned I kept. I was finally my own boss.

I was also attending Santa Monica City College studying economics, accounting, math, and English. A counselor had advised me that taking twelve units and working full time was impossible. But I assured her that nothing was impossible for me. After two years, my plan was to transfer to the University of Southern California and follow an accelerated business course. At the same time, I had every intention of expanding Laila's Nail Studio into a chain. And then, who knows what else?

I had big-time entrepreneurial energy.

I felt driven to make good money and put it back in the black community where it would help change lives. I had dreams.

I also had too much to do. I was running all over town, from Westchester to Santa Monica to Marina del Rey. The counselor turned out to be right; I had bitten off more than I could chew. That first semester I had to drop a course. It took me a while to learn about limitations.

Mike and I were doing well. Our apartment was new and nicely furnished. Our relationship was calm. Our friendship had proven to be real; there was no one I trusted more than Mike.

He and I settled into a good groove. All this was happening in 1996, a year in which two important events transpired. Each had a big impact on my life, though it would take a while to understand exactly how. Seeds were being planted.

In March I was with Alice and a few other friends in Mid-City. We were at her dad's, just hanging out, eating chips and watching TV. Her father had ordered the Mike Tyson–Frank Bruno fight. I'd never been interested in men's boxing unless it was a big-name fight. Before the main bout, though, the announcer talked about a unique event. Two women were fighting. In her first nationally televised pay-for-view appearance, Christy Martin was taking on Deirdre Gogarty of Ireland. I was engrossed. The fight was fierce. Christy got her nose bloodied in the first round but was winning. She looked a mess but continued to fight like a warrior. I experienced a revelation. I saw something I'd never seen before.

At that very moment I wanted to become a

professional fighter.

"I never knew women boxed," I said.

"I didn't know either," said Alice. "This is the first time I've seen it."

"I can do this."

"Do what?"

"Be a fighter."

"Are you serious?"

"Yes."

"You're crazy, Laila," said Alice's dad. "You're not the kind of girl who belongs in the ring. Those women are rough. They'd love to whup a pretty girl like you."

"No one's gonna whup me."

There was no use explaining. I could see why he thought I was crazy. I'd never thought about boxing before. I'd never pursued athletics of any kind. I knew I was naturally strong, but never developed that strength. Everyone thought I was just popping off. But I wasn't. Something deep inside me responded to what I saw on the screen. It was this incredibly focused feeling. I saw myself in the ring. Many months would pass before I acted on that instinct. The seed needed time to grow. But once planted, it sprung roots, roots that went deep.

. . .

That summer my father lit the torch at the Olympics in Atlanta and, just like that, his celebrity increased tenfold. He had never been completely out of the limelight, but something about that moment excited the world and renewed him in spectacular fashion. Suddenly everyone wanted him. He started a nonstop schedule of personal appearances and autograph conventions.

When he had visited L.A. in the past, he might stay at an airport hotel. Now it was a luxury suite at the Beverly Hills. Of course I was happy for him. It was his good karma. He was a genuine hero who, even as his Parkinson's disease became more evident, displayed the same courage that had always marked his character. He made himself available to help others and never tried to hide his condition.

Lonnie was even more in control, supervising his schedule, his diet, his whole life. That was understandable. Now that the offers were pouring in, he needed a trusted cohort to take charge. Lonnie was definitely in charge. She'd often be off in meetings when Hana and I visited Dad in his hotel room. Though he wouldn't talk in front of cameras, he still talked up a storm in private. He'd lecture us on religion or tell us some jokes. You'd never leave without seeing one of his magic tricks. And you were usually recruited into taking notes as he combed the Bible for contradictions. He was still dead set on proving other religions wrong and Islam right.

I'd express my opinion—"don't focus your energy on that; let people believe whatever they believe"—but it'd fall on deaf

Mom and Dad's wedding.

*Mom and Dad when they
were together.*

*My parents, dressed
up for a costume party.*

Photo credit: Howard L. Bingham

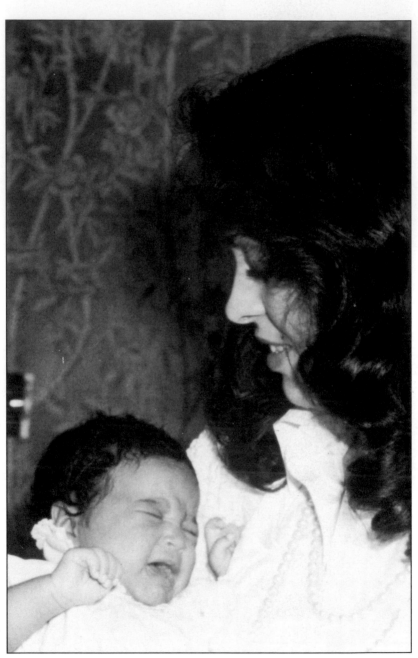

Me as an infant in Mom's arms.

A dinner party at home. Me and Mom are on the right; Hana and Dad are on the left.

In Dad's arms in the backyard, with two friends of the family.

Me (in the center, eating popcorn) with Dad and all my sisters and brothers.

My kindergarten portrait.

My first grade portrait.

*Age 12. Check out my
nerdy glasses.*

*Age 14, and no one could tell me
I wasn't cute.*

*Age 16, hanging
out at a friend's.*

Hana, on the left, and me, in the new millennium.

Mom and her husband Carl.

Overeating at the nail salon, age 19.

Dad, me, Yahya, and Lonnie. My wedding day.

Yahya and me out for the evening.

My 12-year-old stepdaughter, Ebony.

My ninth professional fight, against Christine Robinson.

ears. My father was obsessed with religion. He was obsessed with the notion of Judgment Day. He feared God. He wanted to make sure he was right with God, and there was no way to argue that, from my point of view, fear was not the key to faith. So I left him alone. I also wasn't ready to discuss my epiphany about being a boxer. That might get him upset and, besides, once a seed is planted you don't dig it up to see how it's doing. I'd heard my friends' reaction to my *I-can-do-it* statement. I decided not to talk about it anymore. When the right time came, I was simply going to do it.

My father and I had never fully discussed my run-in with the law. Only one time did he mention it.

"I can't believe you were actually in jail."

"Believe me," I assured him, "I was."

He just shook his head and muttered, "I bet you learned your lesson."

But as far as the case itself or my time in the group home, he never asked many questions. I'm not sure that he, unlike Mom, noticed any change in my character. His main concern was my love life.

"I hear you're living with your boyfriend," he said.

"I am."

"I don't think that's right."

"I've known him for years. In fact, he knows me better than you do. Besides, I'm doing what works for me."

"You're living in sin and that ain't right."

"Dad, you can't come in town every few months and tell me how to live my life. It was Mike, not you, who was there through all the hard times. If you want to meet him, just say so. Don't judge me according to your beliefs."

He took a long pause. He considered what I said. I could see I'd made my point.

"You're right, Laila," he conceded. "I shouldn't tell you what to do. You're a grown woman."

It was a crucial juncture in our relationship, a moment when Dad recognized my autonomy. I appreciated his concession. We found a new respect for each other. A new acceptance. I realized that I couldn't change him any more than he could change me. He spent the rest of the time asking me questions about Mike. Dad genuinely wanted to know about the man in my life.

Sometimes Lonnie would take me along when she went shopping. We bonded over our big size 11 feet. We'd have the salesmen tear up the shoe department at Nordstrom's as we tried on every Ferragamo and Donna Karan in sight. We'd go on for hours. There'd be boxes piled up to the ceiling. She'd buy herself a dozen pair, buy me three or four, and think nothing of dropping a quick $3,000. She also expressed interest in my financial situation and a willingness to help.

"Aren't you trying to do too much with full-time school *and* full-time work? Your grades are suffering."

"I know, but I have to be available for my clients."

"The important thing is your plan to go to USC. That's a major step. Work comes second."

Coming from Lonnie, herself a serious businesswoman, I appreciated the encouragement. At the same time, she just didn't understand my commitment to my business. Lonnie was certain she knew what was best for me.

"Your dad and I want to help you," she said. "I'll call you when I get back to Michigan so we can talk about it."

The statement registered, but I was leery. I preferred not to let them help me. I didn't want to answer to Lonnie. But a few months later, I decided to take a chance and let them help me. That's when they started contributing to my rent, with the condition that I'd cut down my work schedule.

By then, believe it or not, Mike and I had finally broken up and I was on my own. It was a difficult split. Mike was my friend; we'd been through a lot together; we'd grown up together. He was my first lover, the guy who was there when I felt so isolated in Malibu; he'd been there when I was in placement and needed support. Mike always treated me like a lady. But our romance had run out of steam. I was feeling restless and bored. I wanted to start going to the gym and working out. I wanted to be on my own. It was a sad moment, but I realized I was moving in a new direction.

"Can't we work it out?" Mike asked.

"I'm not sure."

"I'm willing to do whatever it takes."

"But the thing is this," I tried to say gently. "I want to see what it's like being alone. It isn't you. It isn't anyone else. It's just me."

Being a gentleman, Mike didn't dog me. He respected me enough to let my decision stand. "If you need anything," he simply said, "just ask."

We parted ways and I moved into a little apartment on the west side of Los Angeles. Lonnie and Dad helped with the rent, but I handled everything else from my own income. Because my business was so demanding, my grades suffered, but I got by. I was serious about transferring to USC.

At my salon I was learning about patience, responsibility, and hard work.

I was also learning deeper lessons in the fine art of listening. It's as much a part of the job as getting the nails right.

Most of the time I liked listening. People told me their problems—with their sex lives, their jobs, their families. They trusted me because I was sympathetic and stayed silent. As I washed and sanitized and soaked their hands in hot water, as I filed and shaped their nails, softened their cuticles, trimmed and buffed and shined and even massaged their fingers, they felt I cared. I did. I loved my work and banked on return business and referrals. I was also amazed by all the drama. Everyone had a story. Everyone seemed to be going through crises.

Among the mostly pleasant customers was the occasional lunatic. One lady—I'll call her Wilma—was wild. She'd come in with a basketful of food—fruit, doughnuts, peanuts, chicken. You name it, she was eating it. She usually arrived an hour late, throwing off my schedule, and, making matters worse, she always had something going on. Her daughter wasn't doing right; her job was too stressful; her husband was missing in action. I just wanted to get the manicure done so I could get to school in time. But Wilma was in no hurry.

"You're putting on these nails," she'd say, "but I'm just going to bite them off. I'm a hopeless nail biter."

"Then why are you having me put on fake nails in the first place?"

"Because they're pretty. But not that shade of white you've picked out. I want eggshell white for the tips."

"I don't have eggshell. This white is virtually the same."

"Can't you go out and get eggshell? I can wait."

"My supplier is on the other side of the city."

"Maybe I want pink. Show me a pink."

I showed a pink.

"That pink's too pink. How about green?"

I showed her two greens. One was too dark, the other too light.

"How about a rose?"

I showed her the only rose in stock. She liked it. But when

I started gluing on the tips, she was certain they were the wrong size.

"They fit," I insisted.

"They're too big. I need a smaller size."

"I know what I'm doing."

"It's all wrong."

"Look, Wilma, *you're* all wrong. You come waltzing in here an hour late, show me no respect, and then start telling me how to do my job. See that sign out there? Says '*Laila's* Nail Studio.' I don't have a boss."

"Just show me another size and maybe another color."

"The only thing I'm showing you is the door."

"You're kicking me out?"

"It's looking that way."

"Okay, okay, please let me stay. I won't say another word."

Fine. I finally got through with her nails but decided that was it. Any more crazy clients and they could find another salon.

Most clients were delightful. Especially Tamare. Tamare was an eccentric business lady with a happy hippy vibe. She was a flower child gone to work in public relations, a sweet lady who was always supportive of me. She wore floral dresses and lots of beads. She loved my manicures and was convinced that my long-term plan of an international franchise was sure to succeed.

· · ·

I was living alone, not seeing anyone. I kept myself superbusy working out my life. Then one day at a pool party I met a handsome guy I'll call Lance. There was a strong attraction between us. He was a financial adviser with his own business. At twenty-nine, he was a decade older than me. He had a shy personality and sweet disposition. We started dating but neither of us wanted to get too involved.

Unfortunately Lance turned out to be a flake. He could never keep a date. So I decided not to take him seriously. I called him whenever *I* was in the mood to see him. I enjoyed his company. We stayed cool for several years. If I met another guy with relationship potential, I'd cut off Lance. And he'd understand. In fact, we became good friends. He'd hear me discuss my romantic prospects and offer up advice. The best part of our relationship was the honesty.

I don't want to give the impression that I had it together when it came to men. I wish I did. I wish I could have spotted and avoided all the phonies who came my way. At the time, I was convinced my radar was foolproof, that I was too sharp to be played.

Wrong.

Round
11

AVOIDING
THE DITCH

It was a year or so after I'd broken up with Mike that a friend and I went to a club to hang out. The club was upscale, the crowd multiracial, the music mellow. There was a private area upstairs with overstuffed blue velvet couches where you could relax before easing down to the dance floor to get your groove on.

It was on the dance floor when I first noticed this guy noticing me. I'll call him Pretender. He was a tall handsome brother in his late twenties—eight or nine years older than me—clean cut and well dressed. I was wearing a white dress with spaghetti straps, some 10 pounds heavier than I am now. This was before I got into shape, but I still turned heads. Anyway, Pretender must have liked what he saw. He followed me from the dance floor to the room upstairs. I thought he was smooth. We'd both been smoking a little weed, and it felt like we were on the same vibe.

"I can tell you have a lot of confidence," he said, "by how you carry yourself."

That got my attention. "Most men are a little intimidated by me."

"That's because you've got it going on."

"Oh, so you feel like *you've* got it going on as well," I said.

"I think so."

He let a couple of seconds pass before asking, "So what do you do?"

"I have a nail salon in the Marina."

"Your own?"

"My own."

"I like that. I have my own business."

"What sort?"

"Medical transportation service. I pick up elderly folks who need rides to their doctors."

It sounded reasonable. As an aspiring entrepreneur, I liked meeting men who fit that category. I liked Pretender's personality; he was well spoken and seemed genuinely interested in my work.

"I get a manicure and pedicure every other week," he said. "May I call for an appointment?"

He was asking for my number. I gave him my business card. A little later he walked me to my car. Unlike many men, he didn't come on strong or seem desperate. He saw I was driving an Expedition.

"I have the same SUV," he said while noticing a dent in my door. "But mine is in the shop."

I missed the subtlety of his remark. Seeing my dent gave him the idea of explaining the absence of his own car, which, it turned out, never existed.

I was glad when he called a couple of days later. We made a date and agreed that, because his car was out of service, I'd pick him up. He asked me to meet him in front of a barbershop.

Pretender looked great, all smiles. As soon as he got in my car, he started rolling a joint. More smoke, less clarity. We floated along on a cloud of easy conversation. He pointed out a house where his mom and dad lived. His own house in the San Fernando Valley was being remodeled. Meanwhile, he was living with his parents. Mom was sociable, but Dad was in a wheelchair and always on Pretender's case. Dad played favorites and preferred Pretender's brother.

"You have siblings?" he asked.

"There are nine of us, but only Hana is my full sister."

"Hana Ali?"

"You know her?"

"Everyone knows Hana. She's Muhammad Ali's daughter."

The business card I gave him didn't carry my last name. Now he knew. But that was okay. Eventually everyone knows. We started spending lots of time together. My friends expressed their concern that we were moving too fast. But I assured them we were just hanging out; everything was cool.

When it came to making moves, Pretender took his time. Like an expert, he played on the strongest feminine weakness: a woman's need to hear how much a man likes her. We can't hear it enough.

He pretended
to like me more than he did—and I went for it hook, line, and
sinker.

If I had any doubts, they were removed by Alice. When I told her who I'd met, she was all excited. "Girl, he's fine. That boy's a baller. He's got money. Better hold on to this one."

I cut off Lance who, from the start, expressed skepticism. "Sounds like he's after something," he suggested.

"Don't be jealous. I'm sure you won't be spending your nights alone."

Pretender got more serious. He sped up the romance and wanted to see me every day. I still hadn't seen his car or house; the repairs were taking longer than he thought. His pager was always blowing up and he never stopped talking on his cell. Meanwhile, I did the driving. I drove him to his office, but he never invited me in. There was always drama with his business. Investors were coming in. Investors were falling out. Was I interested in a $2,500 investment? That very question should have sent up another red flag. My vision, though, was blurred. He might have lacked a house and transportation, but his reefer was never in short supply.

After three weeks, he was dropping me off at work so he could use my car. My coworkers and clients would kid me.

"Looks like Laila's been bit by the love bug. She's losing her common sense."

"I haven't lost anything."

"Then why is that man driving your car? Where's *his* car?"

"Being repaired," I said, using the same line Pretender used on me.

Little by little, I got sucked in. I'm not exactly sure how— or why. I think of myself as hard-nosed. I'm scrutinizing. I can smell bullshit a mile away. But not this time. Rather than avoid it, this time I fell in it.

Pretender's dramas got more dramatic. I hated dealing with his mess, but I sure as hell put up with it. He was on the verge of losing his house in the Valley because of some financial screwup. In L.A., his father didn't want him around. From there he moved in with a friend who owned a townhouse in Inglewood. Turned out, though, his buddy wasn't the owner; his buddy's girlfriend was. After a few incidents where Pretender proved to be an inconsiderate guest, she put him out. Now he had nowhere to go. By then I'd moved into a two-bedroom apartment. I had the room. What choice did I have but to let him stay with me?

Lance couldn't believe it.

"What? He's staying with you? You mean, he's actually moved in?"

"I know I'm tripping."

"He's playing you, Laila. Open your eyes."

Alice and Tiffany were saying the same thing. Mom was concerned. And when Lonnie called and Pretender answered, she wasn't happy at all.

But I didn't want to hear what anyone had to say. I didn't appreciate folks getting in my business. I was dead set on doing what I wanted to do.

And I did. I went to work, went to school, went to the gym. I was slowly getting in shape. I hadn't publicly declared my intention to box, but I hadn't lost the idea. The more I worked out, the more I liked it. Hitting the bag made me feel powerful. Moving around the ring felt good.

Having Pretender around the house all the time felt bad. I wanted him out, on his own, independent like me. I gave him an ultimatum: "Next weekend I'm going to a manicurists' convention in San Francisco. When I get back, you need to be in a place of your own."

When he picked me up at the airport he was holding a bouquet of Casablanca lilies and a beautifully wrapped gift box. "Happy birthday, baby," he said. Inside the box was a gorgeous Coach bag. The leather smelled wonderful. He stayed with me that night. "I found a place," he said. "I'm just waiting for my application to process." I didn't press the issue. Looking back, I see that I felt the need to take care of him.

A month later he still hadn't moved. By this point, I'd become tight with his parents. They loved me. They were convinced I was the best thing that ever happened to their baby boy. "Laila's so sweet," his mom would tell Pretender. "Laila has class. Laila's such a hardworking young lady. You'll never do any better than Laila. You better treat Laila right."

His mom got in the habit of dropping by my place, just to visit. She also came to the nail studio for a free manicure. How could I turn down Mama? Things got outright silly, though, when one weekend Mama showed up at my place. She'd just had an argument with her husband and wanted to know if she and her two grandkids could spend the night. What could I say? They stayed all weekend. I saw where Pretender got his mooching skills. I was miserable.

I was even more miserable when it became evident that Pretender was playing around. I found a woman's bracelet on the floor of my car.

"Who left this here?" I wanted to know.

"I found it at the car wash."

"Come on. I'm not that gullible."

"I don't have to lie to you."

I knew he was a unfaithful lying loser, but I still put up with him.

That evening I heard the voice of an irate woman on his message machine: "I know I'll never see you again, but I want my goddamn bracelet back."

While I was at work, he was cheating with women—and using my car to do it. When I told him he could never use my car again, he rented a car. Weeks later his mother called. "He used my credit card to rent a Cadillac and never returned it. They say I owe $3,000. Where is that boy?"

Pretender was out of control, running the streets. His façade had collapsed.

My patience and denial had collapsed.

He was even cheating his mama. He let it all hang out. One night we went out and were followed by a white woman in a black car. We were being stalked. He denied he knew her. Not only did he know her, he was sleeping with her. He was borrowing money from me every day—$20 here, $50 there—until I didn't have enough to buy the groceries. He was so sneaky that he once tried to get me pregnant by slipping off his condom. As far as supporting me—encouraging my boxing or my work at school or the salon—he offered nothing. It was all about him. When I finally demanded he get a job at Home Depot—I'd seen signs saying they needed help—he surprising me by agreeing. But when his first paycheck came, I got nothing. He never paid me back a single dime, let alone helped me with the rent. All we did was fight.

What takes women so long to see the light? What took *me*

so long? I wasn't stupid or desperate. I knew better. Wasn't I supposed to be sharp? Didn't I know what was going on? All I can say is that I fell in the Ditch. The Ditch is that mysterious place where women end up when they hide from reality. I thought back to those times in Malibu when my mom was living with Walter behind locked doors. My mom's one of the smartest women I know. She's getting her Ph.D. in psychology. She understands human behavior. But all her brainpower didn't keep her from falling in the Ditch. I laughed at her, I mocked her, I called her insane. Then, only a few years later, I repeated the cycle.

I was in the Ditch. And once in, it's hard to find the courage to pull yourself out.

It takes more than everyday drama to get back on solid ground. It takes disastrous drop-dead drama to see the light. My drama came when nine months into this sick relationship this fool came home in the wee small hours. I was probably as disgusted with myself as I was with him. How could any self-respecting woman put up with someone like him? He'd said he was going out to meet one of the guys. That was at ten. Midnight came. Then two, then four. Now it was five in the morning and not a word. When he came waltzing in at five-thirty, I tried to contain my fury. I knew it wasn't the time to confront him. He was probably high or drunk—or both. I told myself to wait till the next day. But I couldn't. Rage got the best of me. Just as he had stripped off his clothes and, naked, slipped into bed, I let him have it. I felt like Oprah Winfrey as Sofia in *The Color Purple* going off on Harpo.

"Who the hell do you think you are? You think you can slide in here smelling like sex and think I'm gonna accept it? Forget it. I'm tired of your bullshit, I'm tired of your lying and cheating. I want your sorry ass out of here."

That's when he exploded. His eyes went wide and caught fire. He flat out assaulted me. He got on top of me, put his hands around my neck, and started choking me. At the same time, he was screaming everything he'd been wanting to say. "You think you're superbitch! You think you're better than me? Well, you ain't shit!" The louder he screamed, the harder he choked. I tried to fight him off, but he was too crazed, too strong. I thought my life was over. I saw the morning paper, ALI'S DAUGHTER KILLED BY CRAZED LOVER. I saw Mom and Hana crying over my grave. I saw I had to do something, so I stopped struggling and tried to relax my body. I decided to play along. With whatever breath I could muster, I whispered, "I'm sorry . . . it's okay . . . I understand." By pretending to be sympathetic, I thought I could get him off me. It worked. Acting saved my life. Finally he released his fingers from my throat and rolled off me. He sighed and closed his eyes. I waited a few minutes before saying I had to go to the bathroom. My real plan was to get the hell out. I wasn't staying with this lunatic a minute longer. I tiptoed into the living room. I was wearing nothing but a sheer shortie nightgown, but there was no time to dress. I found my car keys and turned the door knob. He heard the squeak. *"Come back here, girl!"* he screamed. I bolted; I flew out the door and ran down the stairs. Naked, Pretender flew after me, caught my arm at the bottom of the staircase. I grabbed on to the railing and yelled at the top of my lungs and tried to kick him. He squeezed my wrist until the blood stopped circulating. "Get back upstairs," he ordered. No way I was going back. Lights went on from adjoining apartments. People came to their windows, looking at this naked man attacking this barefoot woman in a flimsy nightgown. My hair was all over my head, mascara running down my cheeks. The craziness of my private life had spilled all over the public streets. Pretender put more pressure on my wrist until I thought it would snap. With my free hand, I tried to scratch his face with my keys. I missed but hit the car alarm instead. Thank God. The noise startled him. He let me go and ran back into the house. I ran to my car and peeled off. By then my nightgown was at my waist, but I couldn't care less. I sped over to Alice's. The next day I realized that, at long last, I'd finally pulled myself out of the Ditch. It took all that.

Round 12

SHAPING

UP

There's physical shape and there's mental shape. For me, mental shape is more important. Getting in mental shape meant cutting off all ties with Pretender. After he flipped out I was able to do that. Pretender was lucky I didn't have him locked up. My position was finally clear: I didn't care if he slept in the street, I never wanted to see his face again.

Friends and clients were amazed at how bad the situation had gotten. They wanted to know why it took me so long to come to my senses. I had the same answer then as now: *It takes as long as it takes.* We all have different learning curves. Having learned the lesson once, though, I swore never to go through it again. I had no intention of getting bit by the same dog twice.

Once my mental situation improved, so did my physical. I could concentrate on training and getting strong. My strongest period came right after my weakest. I wasted no time in getting on with my life. My growth has been erratic and unpredictable.

Just when I thought I was losing it—hooked up with Pretender and unable to cut the fool loose—I found myself free. Freedom came after I hit bottom. Sometimes you have to sink low to rise high. It didn't matter how many family members or friends told me I was heading the wrong way on a one-way street. I had to learn through my own experience.

The Pretender fiasco may have contributed to the intensity of my early training. If I was motivated before, now I was supermotivated. Nothing was going to get in my way. At the same time, another incident added to my motivation. It involved my father's wife.

Lonnie's phone call came out of the blue.

"Your father and I can no longer afford to help you," she said.

"Well, if you can't afford to help me with my rent, how will you be able to send me to USC?"

"We'll cross that bridge when we come to it."

Of course we both knew it was she, not he, who cut me off. I wasn't about to argue because I was never comfortable about taking their money in the first place. At the same time, Lonnie showed little consideration. Here I was with my rent due in ten days and she was withdrawing all help, just like that. I felt that she hurt me more than she helped. No matter what, I wasn't about to go behind her back to Dad. I knew that if I mentioned it to him, he'd come through. But I left it alone.

The incident had a strong impact on me. At the time, I didn't see it as a good thing; now I do. It made me review my plans. I'd been counting on going to USC. USC symbolized my business future. At USC I'd get the sort of education I needed to fulfill my entrepreneurial dreams. But USC was expensive, and without help, out of the question. There was an even greater issue, however.

Because Lonnie had funded me, I realized part of my motivation to attend USC involved her agenda. I'm a person who finishes what she starts, and I had every intention of doing just that. But when Lonnie pulled the rug from under me, I knew this time *my* agenda must prevail. More and more, I was determined to become a professional fighter.

The more I worked out in the gym, the more I was told I had natural ability. My first trainer saw I had speed and agility; he also saw I had heart. In fact, I was eager to get in there and mix it up. I didn't love the rigor of nightly workouts, especially after doing nails all day, but I did it. I was toning up and making progress. I could see the day approaching when I'd actually step in the ring and take on an opponent. That idea excited me.

The competitive part of my personality finally had an outlet, a legitimate way to express itself.

Lonnie's decision to withdraw her help made it clear that self-reliance was my best friend. I'd have to live my life on my own terms. I'd been raised in a household where money was always available. My father prided himself on his good earnings and liked telling us how much he'd make during an autograph convention. He was proud that, unlike so many of his predecessors, he could still make millions simply by being himself.

I thought about the future. Laila's Nail Studio was an ongoing operation. I was loyal to my clientele and they were loyal to me. Customers like Tamare, who encouraged my boxing, were delightful. Many became friends. But I lacked the expertise to go into franchising. I was proud of my success and attached to my salon, yet needed to follow my heart. I was also too practical to deny the obvious: My name was an invaluable aid. If I could develop my skills and put on an exciting athletic performance, the public would pay attention. And besides, it was something I loved.

Other people suggested modeling because I had the looks. And modeling was certainly easier than getting hit in the head. But the truth is that fighting felt right. I wasn't interested in posing half naked in magazines. Besides, boxing was in my blood.

The time came to tell Dad. He was in Los Angeles staying at the Peninsula Hotel in Beverly Hills. When I arrived at his suite, Lonnie had gone to a meeting and Dad was seated in an easy chair, Bible in hand.

"Get a piece of paper," he said. "Got some new inconsistencies I want to remember. Write these down . . ."

I went over and kissed him on the cheek. "Fine, but first I need to talk to you about something."

"Okay."

"I know you've been hearing talk about me boxing. Well, it's true. I didn't want to tell you until I was sure."

I could see he wasn't happy. "Being a fighter isn't easy," he said. "What are you going to do when you get hit upside your head, get all dizzy, and don't know where you are? As my daughter, do you realize the pressure that'll be on you?"

"This is what I want to do, Dad. I'm ready to handle whatever happens."

He paused—I could hear him thinking—before he said, "How are you going to protect your chest? What if you get hit in your stomach and can't have children?"

"We protect our private areas just like men do."

"No matter what you say, Laila, I'm still going to worry about you. You're my baby girl."

"I respect how you feel, Daddy, but I've made up my mind. I'm doing it. I just want you to know, though, that I'll never do it in a way that brings dishonor to you or myself."

For a long time he just looked at me. The silence was loud. What was he thinking? Did I have his support?

I had the answer when he said, "Okay, come over here and show me your left jab."

My mother knew all along. She knew because she and I spoke nearly every day. Our bond was tight. She didn't talk me out of my sick relationship with Pretender any more than I talked her out of Walter, but she was there to listen. Gentleness is one of my mother's great virtues. She bears no malice. She has stuck by her daughters through thick and thin. And, most importantly, her quest for spiritual enlightenment has been a luminous example for us to follow. She has taught us that God is not an abstract theological concept found in books. God dwells within our own hearts, wakes us up in the morning, and guides us along the way. God is our potential for goodness and the good work we do for others. God is unending love, vibrant and alive.

In my mother's life, in the way she overcame obstacles and found peace of mind, I was inspired.

Yet my mother, for all her spiritual serenity, has fears. I felt those fears when I first started talking to her about boxing.

"When I first married your father," she said, "it was difficult to attend his fights. Of course I was proud of him, and of course he was a magnificent athlete. But when you love someone, the last thing in the world you want is to witness their pain. When your husband goes in the ring to face an opponent who's trying to knock him unconscious, you dread the confrontation. Sometimes I had to look the other way. Especially when I knew he was hurt."

"And you don't want to go through the same thing with me."

"It isn't what I want. It's what you want. It's what's right for you. It's just nothing I thought I'd have to go through again."

"Am I making you sad?"

"No. It's just another challenge. It'd be sad, Laila, if you didn't follow your own path. If you're telling me you're certain this *is* the path, then I'll say I'm proud you're pursuing it. I'm proud because, as you know, it isn't an easy path. You'll be under a magnifying glass with a giant spotlight glaring down."

"I know. That's the only part of it I hate."

"That's why it's going to be rough on you. Rough because inevitably you *will* be a celebrity. You're beautiful and talented and I know you'll be one of the best. You have the determination. I've seen you face challenges so I know you're strong. The only way to meet those challenges—when the press is chasing you, criticizing you, characterizing you in ways you don't even recognize—is to believe in yourself.

Your inner strength will get you through.

Round 13

RECOGNIZING

TRUE

ROMANCE

I continued my work—working hard at the nail salon and working out at the gym. It was a grueling routine, but I was determined to achieve both my goals. I didn't have much career guidance and, as far as boxing, I was trying to figure out the business on my own. Everyone had an opinion, but few really understood the game from the inside out. When others urged me to discuss it with my dad, I resisted. I didn't want to lean on him and he had long left the business. Things had changed since his day, and, besides, the world of boxing was a business unlike any other.

All this was on my mind when I attended my father's fifty-seventh birthday in Las Vegas. I had just turned twenty-one and looked forward to what was shaping up as a family reunion. Most of my siblings would be there.

Dad and I were in his suite at the MGM Grand, about to go downstairs for the big dinner, when Hana walked in with two

145

friends. One of the friends was an especially attractive guy. Hana introduced him as Yahya, a Muslim name meaning "The Ever-lasting." I'd later learn his original name was Johnny McClain.

I'd never met Yahya's family, but they all knew my dad. Yahya's mother was there as well. At dinner, Yahya and I were seated at the same table. He kept staring and smiling at me. I didn't respond well. First of all, I wasn't into pretty boys. I could tell he was used to having his way with women. He knew he was fine. I also wasn't used to a guy that good looking being so forward. Usually handsome men play it cool. Even though he was thirty-one, he looked and acted younger. I liked men who acted maturely.

"Yahya likes you," Hana whispered in my ear when the din-ner started to break up.

"Tell him I'm not interested."

"You tell him yourself."

At that moment Yahya came over and said, "How come I've met all your sisters and never met you? I didn't even know there was a Laila."

"Well, I'm usually on my own," I stated standoffishly.

"Maybe we can get to know each other."

"Maybe not." And with that, I walked away.

Next thing I knew his mom was talking to my dad. I over-heard her saying, "My son likes your daughter."

Dad took a bite of ice cream, put down his spoon, and wiped his mouth before replying, "I don't blame him."

Then Yahya appeared and told my father, "I'm going to marry her."

What! I was thinking to myself. *Is everyone here crazy? I just met a man I don't even like and he's talking about marriage. Is some kind of arranged wedding being planned? Have these people lost their minds? This is too weird. I'm going to bed.*

Up in my room, Hana was going on about Yahya. "He's a nice guy," she said. "Give him your number."

"He doesn't interest me."

"He should. You and he have a lot in common. He's a professional boxer.

"Really?"

"Yeah, he was cruiser-weight champ—twice."

Hmmm. I started thinking.

Next morning I was sitting by the pool when here comes Yahya. He couldn't help but notice me rolling my eyes.

"What's that for?" he said.

I decided to be blunt. "Look, you're not my type."

"What's my type? You don't even know me."

"I don't like guys who act like they're cuter than I am."

He laughed and said, "You got me all wrong."

Just then a family acquaintance arrived, an obnoxious man who was half drunk, talking loud and acting the fool. His drink was spilling out of his glass, landing on me. He started wiping my legs with his hands. I cringed. Yahya stopped him dead in his tracks.

"Hold up," said Yahya. "Just move on and leave her alone."

I appreciated Yahya's sensitivity. I was grateful for his quick reaction to an uncomfortable encounter. This was the first time I saw his caring side. He cared that I was being bothered. I felt him protecting me and, for that moment, we bonded.

Later that day, Yahya passed by the registration desk as I was checking out. He smiled and politely asked for my number. I gave it to him.

The very day back from Vegas, I went to the gym, returned to my apartment, and found a message from him on my machine. I was happy to hear his voice and called him right back. "I want to see you," he said. I said it was too soon. He said he just wanted to meet for coffee—tonight. I said I was tired. He kept on insisting. Next thing I know, I'm jumping in the shower, throwing on something cute, and running out the door.

We met at Starbucks in Marina del Rey.

"How do you like your coffee?" the waitress asked him.

"Like my women, light and sweet."

Oh God, I thought, *I made a mistake meeting this guy. That's the dumbest line in the book.*

"I don't consider myself light skinned," I told him.

"Hey, I'm just playing. You take me too seriously. I can tell by the look on your face you care what the waitress thinks. Who cares what she thinks? You know, you have beautiful lips."

"Thank you. You have nice lips as well."

"Thank you. Most people tell me it's my eyes."

"Okay. You're cute, I'm cute. That's been established. Let's move on."

"Hana told me you've been training at the gym."

"Yeah, I'm going to be a professional fighter."

"Who's training you?"

I mentioned a name. "That guy trained me when I was an amateur," he said. "No one's going to take you seriously with him as your trainer."

"You don't need to be worried about that."

The more we talked, the more I couldn't deny that he was fine. And smart. But also silly. Silly men bother me. I like quiet men and Yahya was anything but quiet. On the other hand, he's a Virgo and I'm a Capricorn. Virgo's a soul mate sign to Capricorn. He talked too much, but also had real charm. Try as I might, I couldn't deny that charm. He *did* make me laugh. He *did* make me take myself less seriously. And he *was* interested in hearing about my training. Because he was a champion, I was interested in hearing about his career. At the same time, I wasn't ready for romance.

Besides, Yahya was a Muslim, as was his mother.

I respect Islam, but my childhood experience left a bad taste in my mouth. He also told me he was once married and divorced, and the father of a little girl from a former relationship.

Yahya was persistent. Over the course of several dates, I heard about his many achievements. During the Million Man March, he made up T-shirts and sold them in Washington. He was a concert promoter and brilliant telemarketer. He started his own cable show. He was in the Marine Corps. He'd done it all.

When he sees what he wants, he works to get it.

Because I value that quality in myself, I found it attractive

in him.

One evening Yahya came to the gym to watch me train. He didn't say much; he sat back and observed. He saved his remarks until the ride home.

"I got to be honest with you, Laila. When I first found out about your boxing, I thought it was cute that Muhammad Ali's daughter wanted to fight, but I didn't take you seriously. But now I see you really have a passion for it. The problem is, you've got the wrong trainer. I'll give you an example of why. He hasn't taught you to jab correctly. The jab is the most underrated weapon in boxing. You shouldn't move on to any other lesson until your jab is perfected. Your father could dominate a fight using nothing but his jab."

"I ain't my daddy."

"Just hear me out."

Reluctantly I listened. "You need to learn to use the whole ring," he explained. "When you stand in one spot and slug it out, you get hit with too many punches. A boxer's career doesn't last long, and it lasts even less time when you take too many blows. The key is to train your eyes to see the blows coming—and move your head out the way. Defense is as important as offense."

"It's gonna take a long time to develop that skill," I said defensively. "I'm just getting started."

Yahya showed his frustration with me. "Can you just shut your mouth and open your ears? Stop limiting yourself. If you convince yourself you can't do something, you'll never be able to do it."

The last remark sunk in.

But just when you'd think the brother had said enough, he took it even further. "You're also a little chunky," he added.

"Why don't you tell me how you really feel?"

We laughed, but Yahya was serious. "If you want to be in top condition, you gotta change the way you eat."

That's the last thing I wanted to hear. I love to eat. I figured that since I was working out so hard I could eat whatever I wanted. But Yahya insisted I shed another 15 pounds to enter a weight class where my strength would be an advantage.

"These other girls in the gym aren't dieting," I pointed out.

"You can't compare yourself to them. Just from what I saw today, you're blessed with natural ability. Because of who you are, you have opportunities others don't. If you're not going to put your all into this, you need to change your last name. Get my point? No more fudging."

When Yahya got on his soapbox, he was funny. His words made sense, but he got so worked up I couldn't help but crack up. I was no longer laughing, though, when we went out to eat at an Italian restaurant.

The waiter put down a basket of bread. I love bread. I was in the habit of eating one or two rolls before the salad arrived. I wasn't scared of eating—and eating abundantly—in front of Yahya. It was Saturday night, I'd worked out for four hours that afternoon, and I was starved.

I reached for a piece of buttered-up garlic bread when Yahya actually took it out of my hand.

"Why did you do that?" I asked.

"Look, we've already been through this. Waiter, take away the bread."

"I'll enforce the diet when *I* want to, not you. Waiter, leave the bread."

"Remove the bread."

The waiter's head was bobbing back and forth like a guy at a tennis match. "Take it away," Yahya ordered.

Before the waiter did so, though, I grabbed a piece, looked at Yahya, stared him down, and took a defiant bite. Thus began the War of the Diet.

I remained defiant. I don't like anyone—especially a man—telling me what I can and cannot eat. But Yahya wasn't having it. When I ordered chicken, it had to be skinless. His world was low-fat turkey and protein shakes. He offered himself as an example; he ate like a bird; he was ripped and in top condition. When we started training together—he had a fight in Miami in a couple of months—we'd go on six-mile runs. He'd be up the hill and coming back down—all smiles, barely breaking a sweat—while I was still huffing and puffing my way up. I hated it. I resented him for being so diligent and disciplined. But one thing I couldn't deny.

I was losing weight and feeling good about my progress.

I was feeling comfortable with Yahya. Though he annoyed me with his strong opinions, he understood me. He kept saying he'd never met a woman like me before, and I believed him.

"I'm used to a woman doing what I say. I used to be a playa from the Himalayas," he said in jest.

"Well, you can forget what you're *used to*."

"You sure talk tough."

"You gotta love me or leave me alone."

The quips went on. We were two strong-willed competitors bumping heads. For all the back-and-forth, it led to a friendship that seemed to be deepening. At the same time, only a month after we'd been dating, he made a surprise announcement.

"I don't think either of us should be seeing anyone else."

"Where is this coming from?"

"I just know what I want."

"What makes you think I want the same thing?"

"You know you want me," he said with a laugh. "Seriously, Laila, I really like you. That first night we met I knew I wanted to marry you."

Looking for a little ego boost, I asked, "How did you know?"

"You had quiet confidence. I was attracted to your don't-mess-with-me attitude."

I needed time to think. Usually it's the woman who wants commitment.

The woman wants monogamy; the man wants options.

This man, though, was going the other way. I couldn't help but be impressed. At the same time, wasn't all this happening too soon? Besides, I was doing just fine with Lance who, after the Pretender went off, was back in the picture.

"He's getting too serious too soon," said Lance when I mentioned what was happening.

"I do have feelings for him," I admitted. "Strong feelings."

"Give it some time. What's the rush?"

"I don't think I want to lose him."

"And seeing someone else now and then means losing him?"

"I think so."

"Wait a minute, Laila," Lance cautioned. "You aren't going to wind up marrying this man, are you?"

"I'm not even thinking about marriage. I'm just trying to decide whether I want the relationship to be exclusive."

"I just hate to lose you again. We've got a good thing going."

I thought about it for a few days and came to this conclusion: *the good thing's about to come to an end.*

It wasn't easy kicking Lance to the curb. By then we'd become friends. Given our history, though, I knew the friendship couldn't endure in the light of new romance. He was upset, but he understood my commitment. I told him I hoped he could find a woman to whom he could commit as well. We haven't talked to each other since.

The romance, the training . . . everything about my life intensified.

Yahya had a house in the San Fernando Valley, the last place I wanted to live. It was far from my salon in the Marina and far from the downtown gym where I trained. Besides, I couldn't stand the heat. I didn't even want to visit the Valley, much less live in it. Yet little time passed before I wound up staying there with Yahya.

We continued to squabble. I continued to be put off by his personality. In restaurants, for example, if a song he liked came over the speakers, he might start singing; he might even get up and start dancing. He was free that way and, to my mind, foolish. "Be cool," I'd always tell him. "You're too uptight," he'd always tell me. He didn't care what people thought. I probably cared too much. Ultimately we balanced out—I made him a bit more thoughtful; he made me a little more relaxed—but it took a while.

The first big challenge came in the form of his fight in Florida. I'd never seen him in action before. At the time, Yahya had also begun acting. He was taking lessons and doing commercials, preparing a transition from one career to another. This was a big fight, and I was eager to watch. We flew to Miami together. I sat ringside and studied his every move. Early on, it became clear he was doing too much moving and not enough boxing. After a few rounds, I could see he didn't want to take any chances. I've seen that same attitude in other guys in the gym. Now Yahya had it. I wasn't surprised when he lost the fight by decision, but I was disappointed. Deeply disappointed.

Afterward, in his dressing room, I couldn't even look him in the eye.

"What's the matter?" he wanted to know.

This wasn't the time to describe my disillusionment. I tried to hide my feelings, but couldn't. I've never been good at hiding my feelings.

"Why do you have that expression on your face?" he asked.

"I can't believe you ran around the ring like that. What happened to all that talk about taking your opponent apart?"

He paused to wipe his forehead with a towel. "Look," he said, "it ain't in me anymore."

"I don't get it."

"After the bell rang and he hit me, I realized I didn't want to be punched in the face. I started thinking about my looks and my acting career."

"Then you don't need to be in the ring."

"That's exactly my point. I'm done."

That night he made a decision. He was proud of his twenty-year career that he'd forged on his own. Yahya never had a promoter or made a lot of money. He'd made his own breaks and fought his way to the top using his own smarts and skills. Now those same smarts were telling him to be cautious and ease out of the game without risking his future.

I had to respect him for that.

From then on, everything changed. His focus became my boxing career, not his.

"You can be the future of women's boxing," he said. "That means developing you as the number-one woman fighter in the world. I know this game inside out. I never had the opportunities you have. Now I want to pass down all my knowledge to you, Laila, so you can make history."

Round
14

GOING
FOR IT

I was moving ahead. On Yahya's recommendation, I got a new trainer, Dub Huntley, who'd worked with a number of top fighters. Meanwhile, Yahya convinced me to postpone my professional debut, claiming I needed more work. He was right. Patience is not my strong suit, but slowly I was learning its importance.

We decided early on not to have amateur fights because the system could be political. You can win or lose, not based on skills but on the whims of judges or elements beyond your control. My dad has never gotten involved in my career, but he did make one point very clear: "Don't be exploited. Get what you deserve."

My first fight finally came on October 8, 1999, at the Turning Stone Casino Convention Center in Verona, New York. I started out as a pro, a 165-pound super middleweight. I trained to the max and shed every last inch of fat. I was ready. Members of the press wondered if my dad would attend; rumors were circulating that he was against my career. I knew he was coming, but I kept the press guessing. Along with Dad, Mom and Hana were there to support me.

The fight ended before it began. I was ready for a competitive bout and disappointed when it was no contest. But I was happy I won. I hardly got hit—except for a sucker punch thrown by the critics.

The critics complained that my first opponent wasn't ready, that April Fowler worked as a waitress. Well, I worked as a manicurist. Ninety-nine percent of women boxers have day jobs. They don't get the exposure that would let them earn a living as fighters. Besides, it was hardly my fault that I dominated my first bout. Yahya chose an opponent who, like me, had limited experience. As a beginner, it seemed fair to fight another inexperienced fighter. Yahya was adamant about keeping me off TV until my skills had developed. I needed to start somewhere and was grateful I started out a winner. The press viewed it cynically, calling it a publicity stunt.

At first that bothered me. But I soon saw that the press would always be negative, no matter what I said. They courted me because I was news. They liked my celebrity name and said I was pretty. But they resented me and looked for ways to discredit my achievements. Like a two-faced friend, the press loves and hates with equal passion. I learned to accept that reality. Unlike my father, I had no quips or witty remarks. When I spoke to the press, I was straightforward. I told myself early on, *This is the game I've chosen to play and, like it not, criticism is part of it.*

My clients got caught up in my new celebrity, many discovering for the first time I was Ali's daughter. The phone was ringing off the hook. Men were making appointments just to meet me. It drove me crazy. I battled with the decision to continue running Laila's Nail Studio. Throughout my training and beyond my first fight, I managed to stay on top of my business. But after that initial bout, it became harder. For months Yahya had urged me to close down the shop, yet I resisted.

"You don't know how hard I've worked to build my business," I'd say.

"Sure I know," he'd answer. "But to be a serious athlete you have to be 100 percent focused on boxing."

I knew he was right. But I also knew the tremendous effort required to get my license and build my business. I'd begun working during a troubled time in my life—when I needed financial and emotional relief. I couldn't help but get emotional when I considered closing that chapter. Loyal customers like Tamare had become dear friends. My salon symbolized my independence and endurance; to the very end, I took pride in my work. But now priorities were shifting.

Despite the criticism surrounding my first fight, writers were drawn to the larger story:

Ali's daughter is putting on the gloves.

I saw that my initial instincts were right. I earned $35,000 for my professional debut when other female fighters were earning $200 a round. But I never disclosed my earnings when the press asked; I didn't want to flaunt it in front of the hardworking women who'd paved the way before me. I was motivated to prove I wasn't a gimmick; I was a bona fide athlete. Now I saw how Yahya was right;

to become a world-class fighter would require my undivided attention.

So I made the decision to quit doing nails. I wrote to each of my customers, thanking them for their patronage and regretting I could no longer manage two careers at the same time.

Four weeks later, I won again, this time by technical knockout (TKO) in the fourth round. I was gaining confidence. My victories mounted. In Detroit, a couple of weeks before my twenty-second birthday, I knocked out Nicolyn Armstrong in the second round. On March 7, 2000, I knocked out Crystal Arcand in the first.

My next fight was tougher. My opponent was Karen Bill. She was physically big. After the press conference announcing the event, I remember going to the bathroom where an attendant said, "That girl looks tough. Aren't you worried?"

I laughed it off. Sure she looked tough, but I knew looks didn't mean anything. I was ready. We fought before ten thousand fans at Joe Louis Arena in Detroit. My father attended. Round one had me moving around. I'm not a fast starter; I first want to see what my opponent has got. In the second round I landed some shots but got hit with an uppercut that knocked me down for the first and only time in my career. When I got up before the ref could begin the count, it was obvious I wasn't hurt. But I knew Karen thought I was dazed; I knew she was coming after me. Yahya yelled, "Get on your toes, Laila, and move around the ring!" But my inexperience and inner toughness made me go to war. I had to whup her ass. I started landing powerful combinations that backed her up and bloodied her face. The ref stopped the fight in the third round because Karen looked dazed. I was declared winner by TKO. Karen protested, claiming she was ahead when the fight was stopped. I agreed that the ref could have let it go. I was disappointed that I didn't have the chance to knock her out cold. If you look at the tape, though, I clearly won.

"She was strong," Dad said to me after the fight. "Were you worried when she knocked you down?"

"Not really. You saw how I put it on her."

"Girl, you bad."

Given my father's penchant for praising people, I accepted his compliment but didn't let it go to my head.

A month later, I was off to China to fight Kristina King. Yahya felt I was ready to handle the pressure of a televised bout. The event was broadcast back home, and I won by TKO in the fourth.

I'd always wanted to fight in my hometown, and now it was time. I wanted my family and friends to see me in action. Yahya got his promoter's license and started his corporation Absoloot Boxing. He put the event together at the Universal Ampitheater, a first for that venue. The naysayers said it would fail. The naysayers were wrong. The setup was ideal and the fans loved it. Yahya developed a good card, with five strong opening bouts. I was upset, though, when my opponent backed out at the last minute. Suddenly all prospective opponents were asking outrageous amounts because they knew we were desperate for a replacement. He finally got a woman, Marjorie Jones, whose record made me argue for a tougher challenger. But it was too late. The fight was two days off.

It was at the press conference when I learned Marjorie was forty-eight. I thought I'd die. I knew the press was going to tear me apart. Embarrassed, I threatened to back out, but finally came to my senses. I wasn't going to jeopardize Yahya's production. I accepted a fact of life: At some point, every fighter faces a mismatch. I wasn't surprised that I knocked her out, only disappointed that it came sixty-eight seconds into the first round. I didn't feel like a winner. I felt ashamed, but happy the fans loved the event. Dad was in the front row along with Will Smith and other celebrities. My record climbed to 7–0.

With each fight I was convinced I'd chosen the right career path. I developed a routine that worked: I talk to myself in the dressing room: *I've trained harder; I'm stronger; I'm better; the blood of a champion runs through my veins; I've earned this opportunity; I'll earn this victory; I've already won.*

I'm focused. There's no room for nervousness. This is what I've been working for.

When my hands are wrapped, my gloves are on, and I start hitting the mitts, I'm pumped and ready to devastate my opponent. I calmly wait for the knock on the door. The knock comes and I'm glad. I move toward the moment of truth.

Climbing into the ring, I begin hearing the cry of "Ali! Ali!"— the same cry that greeted my father so many years before. The energy from the crowd brings tears to my eyes.

I think of my potential as a role model

for young women— especially young black women— looking for positive guidance and personal

strength.

As I greet my opponent in the center of the ring, I look dead in her eye and stare deep into her soul to see what she's made of. In my eyes there's not the slightest hint of fear. I can't be intimidated. We go to our corners, the bell sounds, and it's on and cracking.

I love the give-and-take, reading an opponent's body lan-

guage, anticipating a punch before it's thrown. I see the foot-
work, the motion, the dance in my dreams. I love the subtle
play between defense and offense, jabbing and ducking, moving
ahead, maintaining position, giving ground, gaining momentum.
I live to get out there and trade punches and go for the knockout. Early on, I see how my aggressive stance is both good and
bad—good because it expresses my natural bent as a fighter;
bad because at times it has me brawling rather than boxing.
Being unafraid and aggressive isn't enough; mastering the skills
is what makes a fighter complete.

Sometimes the press painted me as arrogant. I wasn't. It's
just that confidence can be confused for cockiness. I knew I was
the best at my level. As my reputation grew, other female fighters expressed resentment. I understood why: I was getting more
attention and money than women with more experience. I wish
all female boxers were better paid, but what they didn't realize
was that I was helping everyone by bringing attention to the
sport. I could do so because of my talent and my name.

Yahya always made it clear he wanted to get married. That was
his message from the start—"I'm a one-woman man, and you're
that woman." When he started talking about engagement, I jok-
ingly said, "I'll marry you when you show up with a three-carat
ring."

"So that's what it's going to take?"

"I've got a big hand. I need a big rock."

A few weeks later we went to visit my father in Michigan. Dad said he welcomed the chance to get to know Yahya better. When we arrived, though, the vibe was weird.

"Look, Laila," Lonnie said to me just after we arrived. "It's not a good idea for you and Yahya to stay at the house. He should stay at a hotel."

"That doesn't make any sense. We live together," I reminded Lonnie.

"Your father's not comfortable with you sharing a bedroom here."

"We were going to sleep in separate rooms out of respect anyway, but we'll just go to a hotel."

"He won't be pleased that you're sharing a hotel room."

"Isn't this kind of silly?"

"Not to a man of your father's religious convictions."

I held my tongue because I planned to discuss it with Dad— privately. He could tell me how he felt himself.

When Yahya and I had our talk with my father, his attitude was much different than the one Lonnie represented.

"It's your business what you do," he said. "I just can't condone you guys sleeping in the same bed under my roof until you're married."

Yahya understood and assured him he had plans to marry me. As Muslims, Yahya and my father bonded over the importance of commitment and matrimony.

Yahya formally popped the question at our favorite restaurant, Crustaceans in Beverly Hills. I had picked out the ring a few days before; it was just what I wanted. By then we'd been together a little over a year. Never before had I felt the kind of love Yahya extended to me. After struggling with the relationship, I surrendered. We were together practically every minute of every day. There were no secrets. His pager, his cell phone, his voice messages—his life was an open book with no hidden agendas. It took me a while to see the degree of his sincere devotion. My well-earned skepticism didn't dissipate overnight. But when that last degree of doubt did disappear, I felt relief. I felt like I was finally facing the truth: I found the good man I deserved, my soul mate.

Not everyone respected my relationship with Yahya. Alice was especially insensitive to my feelings. She always found something derogatory to say about my fiancé. If she thought I would choose her over Yahya, she was wrong. What woman in her right mind wants to hang around a friend with that kind of negative vibe? If you're not respecting my relationship, you're not respecting me. I told Alice all this in no uncertain terms. I invited her to the wedding, but I wasn't surprised when she never replied or attended. I was sad to see this longtime friendship fall apart over nothing.

But I was entering a new phase,

and there was no room for negativity.

Meanwhile, Yahya and I had a wedding to plan. It wasn't easy. We had different views on the matter.

"I want a small private wedding," I said.

"I want all our family and friends there," he said.

As much as I didn't want to be on stage, I caved in. The wedding was stressful. Two days before the big event we'd just moved into our first house. I was uptight. Originally the ceremony was going to be on a yacht, but those plans collapsed. Then I hired a wedding planner, but she was a disaster. I wound up doing the planning. It was huge—250 invited guests at the Ritz-Carlton Huntington Hotel in Pasadena, pictures in *People* magazine, the whole nine yards. Like most brides, I was an emotional mess. Everything had to be perfect. I was up till dawn the night before writing out place cards. On the day itself I was too preoccupied to really enjoy it. I wore a white fitted gown encrusted with tiny crystals. Everyone looked beautiful and called it the classiest wedding they had even seen. Yahya looked more handsome than ever. I began to feel calm—that is, until it was time to walk down the aisle with Dad.

I saw a side to my father I'd never seen before. He seemed a little fearful. Before we took a step, he asked me over and over, "What side should I stand on? Do I hold your hand? How fast should I walk?" I took his hand and assured him it was all going to be all right. I told him I would lead the way. When we heard the strains of Jill Scott's "He Loves Me," he could barely move. His arms were extremely heavy; he felt like a brick. I practically had to pull him down the aisle. This man, who had fought before millions of screaming fans all over the world, was now nervous. I accompanied him down the aisle and then guided him to his seat. He was so flustered he forgot to remove my veil. I did it myself and kissed him on the cheek. Reverend Michael Beckwith of Agape, the Science of the Mind church favored by my mother and me, officiated. His service was deeply spiritual. My stepfather Carl Anderson sang "Ribbon in the Sky" so movingly there were few dry eyes when he was through. Yahya and I stood under the flowered altar and gazed into each other's eyes. Suddenly everyone and everything disappeared. We were in our own world, our eyes filled with tears, relishing the moment.

Round
15

STEPPING

OUT ON

FAITH

t was a big card, a pay-for-view event at $49.95 a pop, with Mike Tyson versus Andrew Golota as the main attraction at The Palace in Auburn Hills, Michigan. My opponent was Kendra Lenhart, a 6-foot-2 veteran with a reputation as an especially hard hitter. I looked forward to confronting her.

My father showed up at my dressing room just before the fight. It was quiet time, the last moments of reflection before the battle begins. Dad gave me a big hug and looked me in the eye. He saw I was ready. He liked seeing I had that same confidence he had demonstrated his whole life.

"I'm fighting another big girl," I said.

"Bigger they come, harder they fall."

He kissed me on the cheek and left.

The stare-down let me know Kendra wasn't intimidated by me. And when the bell rang, she came out swinging. Her flailing blows, raining down from over my head, were hard to block.

In the second round, she hit me with a punch that rocked me. By round three, I'd caught on to her game. I began connecting with a stiff hard jab that knocked her off balance. Over the course of the fight, I broke her down by hitting her with hard body shots. This was the first fight where I felt like my competitor matched my strength, forcing me to use strategy, not just punching power. The fight went the six-round distance, and I won an unanimous decision.

In reviewing the tape, I heard how commentators reveal their bias about women's boxing. Before the fight they said Kendra was a tremendous athlete in top condition. When she began weakening after a few rounds, they concluded that she hadn't been in good shape after all. Well, the truth is, she *was* in good shape; it was my body shots that slowed her down. If it were men fighting, the commentators would have reported it more accurately.

As my notoriety grew, it became more of a challenge to think of myself as a celebrity. I was expected to attend premieres and parties. I didn't have the quick smile and easy quip that such events require, which is why I often declined. I'm just not Hollywood. At the same time, when I chose to box I knew my life would become public.

I knew I had
a responsibility to be a positive
role model.

I found there were better ways to give back to my fans than showing up at flashy parties. I favored low-key talk shows and charity events for legitimate causes.

Sometimes I think people (and the press) expect me to be a charismatic entertainer like my father. But I'm just me. I do what comes naturally. If I'm in a happy mood, I smile; if I'm in a talkative mood, I talk; but if I'm in private mood, I keep quiet.

Kids are an exception. I always give children attention, especially little girls. When kids ask for my autograph, I stop what I'm doing and give them all the time they want. I make a point of telling little girls that they're pretty and write "stay beautiful" on their autographs. If a little girl is chubby or less than picture perfect, I stress how beauty comes from within. People don't realize that the images they see on television—women with perfect bodies—are illusions. It's all makeup, plastic, and costumes. My belief is that self-esteem is more valuable than anything the eyes can behold.

My strongest support has come from the black community. My people have embraced me with great generosity. Wherever I travel, walking through airports or malls, shopping the supermarkets or buying gas, they always encourage me. "Keep doing what you're doing, Laila. You make us proud." Many of them aren't even boxing fans, but show love and respect for me because they see I'm real. Their attitudes constitute a tremendous support system that keeps me aiming even higher.

I was recently invited to Japan to witness an Ultimate Fighting Event, one of those brutal bouts that can match a wrestler against a kick boxer. When the bout was over, the promoters offered me a lot of money to fight the winner. I refused because I'm a boxer, not a wrestler. Besides, it would make both me and women's boxing look bad.

Some critics accuse me using my looks to get ahead. That's hard to understand, since I don't work at looking pretty in the ring. In the ring it's all about winning. There are some women boxers, of course, who wear makeup and skimpy outfits when they fight. They have that right; I don't judge them. Besides, they aren't stealing my shine. If I start worrying about what they're doing, I'll lose my focus. My eye is on those championship belts.

I understand the importance of publicity. When the Dairy Farmers Association asked me to pose with my father for their "Got Milk?" campaign, I agreed. I chuckled at the caption they wanted to use, "Father knows best," and looked forward to posing with a milky mustache. The photo shoot, though, wasn't easy. Dad was tense. The problem was my outfit. He knew Muslims throughout the world would be seeing this picture. Annie Liebowitz, the famous photographer, had me in a tank top to reveal my athleticism. But my father didn't care about her concept; he wouldn't take the picture until I changed into a long-sleeved shirt. At first he also refused to be smeared with milky mustaches.

"It makes it look like we were kissing," he said.

"No it doesn't," I insisted. "Everyone knows these ads are about drinking milk."

The ad came out and proved a big favorite with both his fans and mine.

My success in boxing inspired Joe Frazier's daughter Jacqui. She'd been running her mouth about how she could beat me. Jacqui was thirty-nine, I was twenty-three. She had less experience in the ring than me and, to be honest, I didn't see her as a serious opponent. But because our fathers had fought three legendary fights in the seventies—Joe won the first, my dad the next two— I couldn't deny the public interest. The higher the interest, the higher the pay. Besides, my advisers were saying that this fight would take women's boxing to another level. Regardless of my feelings about Jacqui's self-serving motivations, I had to do it.

Jacqui and I held joint press conferences, did joint interviews, posed together for the cover of *TV Guide*. She loved her newfound stardom and said whatever she thought sounded good. From the first time I met her, I didn't like her. Her banter was insincere. Her babbling disgusted me. She talked trash about how she would help me up off the canvas after knocking me on my butt. My reply was simple: "Just work on your skills, girl, so we can give the people their money's worth." I didn't want her fighting so wild that she'd make me look bad.

I prepared vigorously. Weeks before the fight, I went to camp high in the mountains of Big Bear Lake, California. The routine was rugged. Up at 5 A.M. for a five-mile run. Work out in the gym with the heavy bag, then the speed bag, climb in the ring with two male sparring partners for four rounds each. Jump rope. Hit the floor for four hundred sit-ups. Keep to a strict diet. In bed by nine. Up at 5 A.M.—and start all over again.

The fight, copromoted by Absoloot Boxing, happened June 8, 2001, at the Turning Stone Casino in Verona, New York, the same venue where I had begun my career exactly twenty months earlier. Yahya had managed my career with consummate skill. I was 9–0 with eight knockouts. He refused the fight with Jacqui early on because the timing was wrong. But now interest was high. For the first time in history, a woman's bout was the top attraction of a pay-for-view event. Journalists came from all over the world. I was determined to demonstrate my fighting prowess in front of the largest audience I'd ever drawn.

My father, who couldn't attend, called me just before I went into the ring.

"You know she's coming out swinging," he said. "Don't get caught up in that. Just box."

Then the moment of truth:

It was time to face eight thousand fans, five hundred reporters, and a worldwide TV audience.

My father was right; she came out freewheeling and wild. She was crazily aggressive. In the first round, she hit me with a few grazing punches that were ineffective. But she threw me off my game plan. Once again, instead of boxing, I slugged it out.

The crowd loved the excitement. The emotions were real. We both wanted to win. In the third round, I stepped it up and started hitting with powerful combinations. Jacqui was in trouble. If she hadn't spit out her mouthpiece to delay the fight, I would have knocked her out. As the fight went on, she held on for dear life. Jacqui was tough. She took the punches and displayed courage.

After eight action-packed rounds, I won a majority decision.

The fans were more than satisfied. And women's boxing benefited. Suddenly a new audience was born. At the postfight press conference, I was honored to introduce Jackie Tonawanda, a female boxing champ and friend of my father's who had dominated the ring back in the late sixties and early seventies. Tonawanda is a pioneer who paved the way for young women like me. She was happy to see her sport reach a new level.

Reaching.

I'm still reaching. I'll keep fighting until I win a championship. If I wake up one morning and decide to stop boxing, though, I will. I'll continue to live my life day by day.

In my eyes, the world is like a clean canvas.

I can mix the colors and paint my picture a hundred different ways.

I'm interested in community service—helping single mothers who need day-care facilities, putting entrepreneurial energy back in black neighborhoods, encouraging people to realize their potential.

I began this book by saying that wisdom must come from our own stories. If you don't understand your own story, you'll wander through life lost. I also said my story is about reaching your potential and getting strong. It's also about staying true to yourself.

I believe God has given each of us a unique quality. Who we are, what we say, how we act, what we do—it all comes out of our life experiences. We should all accept our differences, which ultimately means respecting the gift God has given us.

Reaching for that gift will lead to personal power and pride, qualities that enable us to overcome all obstacles.

I offer my story as an example of someone willing to reach beyond circumstances she didn't like.

I stand as an example of someone who grew stronger by taking responsibility for herself.

I don't mean to say others haven't helped me, because they have. My mother is a shining example of spiritual strength. My dad is a man who exudes kindness and love. My husband is my heart, my wise counselor, my best friend.

Ultimately, though, personal power—love and respect for yourself—must be of your own making.

If you want to lose weight and get in shape, stop procrastinating; get up and do it.

If you want to go to school and get a degree, be ready to put in the effort.

STEPPING OUT ON FAITH

If you want to be a positive person, let go of the negative characters holding you down.

Don't let your past define you.

Our stories have long and sometimes unhappy histories behind them, but you can start fresh every morning.

Every morning I wake up with God's love inside of me.

I know that love is real.

Just as I know my story is just beginning.

And so is yours.

A POEM

FOR LAILA

BY

HANA ALI

Times are hard and the streets are rough,
this is why I'm forced to act so tough.
My skin is brown, though I lived that down,
this is how I was caught in a circle of frowns.
My legs stand tall but my arms reach short
this is how I missed the grasp of support.
My mind is strong and my intentions never wrong
but I always seem to sing the same sad songs.
One thing I've realized is life isn't long.
So from here on I'll do no wrong.
I'll stand tall with my head held high.
My frown will rise, my eyes will shine.
Because now I see that the prize is life
and I intend to reach my palace in the sky.
So on my journey to a better place,
I'll keep all the memories of yesterday.
Now born again with much left to defeat,
only this time around my mind will compete
and no more storms will knock me to my knees
because this time around I have surfaced my feet.
I'll blow a breeze with a breath of ease
to then live my life with unending peace.